LONDON'S
ENGINE SHEDS

Volume 1. The West and North

ROGER GRIFFITHS & JOHN HOOPER

Copyright Book Law Publications – First published in the United Kingdom in 2017

ISBN 978-1-909625-68-6

Printed and bound by The Amadeus Press, Cleckheaton,West Yorkshire
Published by Book Law Publications, 382 Carlton Hill, Nottingham, NG4 1JA

Introduction

The history of London's steam sheds dates from 1836, through to the end of main line steam working in the Capital in July 1967, although London Transport's small fleet of steam locomotives worked on until 1971. In the course of those 135 years, around one hundred and thirty engine sheds and principal locomotive stabling points served the railways of Greater London, but by the period of British Railways in the 1950s – inevitably the era most favoured by latter-day enthusiasts – that number was much reduced. Thus, in putting together a photographic reminder of Greater London's steam sheds, only the days of British Railways will be covered and with the few remaining stabling points being ignored, your authors are left with just eighteen "main" sheds to feature – too many, however, to adequately do justice in a single volume.

Fourteen terminal stations served the Capital and if you ask a non-enthusiast how many were situated south of the River Thames, some might be surprised when they hear just two: London Bridge and Waterloo. Therefore the majority of engine sheds was also to be found north of the Thames, which gave the authors a problem of subdivision – we simply could not just compile two volumes: North London and South London, with the Thames being the dividing line. Accordingly, working first on the north bank, in a clockwise direction, Volume One will cover the area west and north of the city, where in pre-Grouping terms, were sheds of the: LSWR (1); GWR (2); GCR (1); MR (2); LNWR (2) and GNR (2) – total 10 depots. Volume Two will feature East London (still north of the river) and London, south of the Thames.

What follows can give only a flavour of what London was like in the heady days of (nearly) all-steam working; helping us to create that flavour were a number of individuals and organisations including the Armstrong Railway Photographic Trust, David Dunn, Norman Preedy, Chris Dunne who allowed us to use his father's original notes created during shed visits in the 1950s and 1960s. Finally, Peter Hands provided useful information from his revised *What Happened to Steam* series. Thank you all.

Roger Griffiths, North Cyprus
John Hooper, Manche, France

Front Cover :   A3 No.60066 MERRY HAMPTON, A4 No.60026 MILES BEEVOR, and A3 No.60047 DONOVAN grace the yard at King's Cross engine shed in September 1961. *Transport Treasury.*

Back Cover :   (*Top Picture*) See Page 19. (*Bottom Picture*) See Page 91.

Frontispiece: Ivatt Class 2 No.46509 at Willesden 8th January 1965. *K. Gregory.*

FELTHAM

Feltham engine shed was constructed in 1922, the last year of the London & South Western Railway's (LSWR) existence. At opening it was the base for some 80 locomotives that provided motive power for the huge new, Feltham marshalling yard, where freight traffic was received from the south coast ports and West of England, to be sorted and despatched in cross-London workings to numerous destinations around the Capital.

Constructed in concrete, Feltham depot was of six through roads under a northlight roof with a single road repair shop along one side. The shed was provided with a 65 foot turntable and one of the few mechanical coaling plants employed by the LSWR and its successor, the Southern Railway (SR). Coded FEL by the SR, the depot was re-coded 70B by British Railways (BR), Southern Region and saw its first diesel shunting engines in 1954. The intention was for Feltham to continue past the end of steam as a diesel shed, but that was not to be, so the depot closed on 9th July 1967. Today the shed's site is covered by Heathrow Gateway industrial units.

A nice impression of Feltham's concrete engine shed seen from the east, on Saturday 17th October 1959. The four locomotives on view were, from left to right: Class S15 (Maunsell) 4-6-0 No.30832 (Eastleigh, October 1927), which was visiting from Salisbury, at which depot it would remain until being withdrawn in January 1964; Class N, 2-6-0 No.31892 (Eastleigh, January 1931), had arrived at Feltham, from Faversham in May 1959, and would move on to Tonbridge in June 1960; eleven months later it transferred to Three Bridges, where it was withdrawn in November 1962. Class H16 No.30516 (Eastleigh, November 1921) and her sisters are discussed in more detail in a later caption; this particular 4-6-2T would remain at Feltham until withdrawal in November 1962; finally Class S15 (Urie) 4-6-0 No.30498 (Eastleigh, April 1920), which had been based at Feltham for many years and be withdrawn from there in June 1963. *Norman Preedy.*

Feltham – What was on shed Sunday 25th May 1952:

30038, 30043, 30230, 30254, 30339, 30346, 30355, 30352, 30488, 30492, 30493, 30495, 30497, 30499, 30500, 30501, 30503, 30504, 30505, 30508, 30509, 30510, 30512, 30514, 30515, 30516. 30517, 30521, 30523, 30567, 30568, 30569, 30570, 30571, 30572, 30687, 30688, 30689, 30696, 30697, 30744, 30834, 30839, 30840, 33006, 33010, 33011, 33012, 33013   Total: 49.

Part of Feltham's marshalling yard is seen around 1950, with Class G16, 4-8-0T No.30492, employed on hump shunting duties, for which the four members of the class (BR 30492 to 30495), were specifically designed by Mr. Urie in 1921. Weighing-in at just over 95 tons the G16 were reputedly the widest locomotive to be employed in Britain, but this did not stop them from making occasional forays, working trips along London's western circle line, to Neasden and Cricklewood. Note that at the time the 4-8-0T still sported SOUTHERN on its side tanks; it would be withdrawn from Feltham in January 1959. *Ken Cockerill (ARPT).*

A second type of large tank engine was designed by Urie for the Feltham yards, but the five members of the H16 class were specifically for working cross-London freights. The 4-6-2 tanks were really mixed traffic engines though and in later life, when they had not so much work from Feltham, they could be seen on such duties as empty carriage stock working at Waterloo. Numbered under BR 30516 to 30520, engine No.30518 (Eastleigh, December 1921), is nicely posed in front of Feltham engine shed at an unknown date, but probably in the mid-1950s. All five H16 would move to Eastleigh depot in January 1960, only to return to 70B, *en masse,* in May 1961. The quintet would be withdrawn during the last two months of 1962. *W.R.E. Lewis (ARPT)*

In BR times the bulk of Feltham's freight traffic was typically handled by Class S15, 4-6-0, and 0-6-0s of classes 700, Q and Q1, but even then elderly types from the LSWR period still could be seen, up to the late 1950s. One such 'old lady' is seen here at Feltham on Thursday 25th August 1955. Class 0395, 0-6-0, No.30570 had emerged from Nine Elms Works in May, 1883, but at 72 years old still looked to be in good condition – in fact she would survive until the end of 1956. Behind 30570, an un-lovely, but very powerful 0-6-0 of Bulleid's Class Q1 looks on; No.33026 (Ashford, July 1942), had been a Feltham engine since September 1953 and would move on, to Three Bridges in September 1962, return in December 1963 and then transfer twice more: in November 1964 to Guildford and May 1965 to Nine Elms, where it ended service five months later. *C.W. Allen (ARPT)*

Another aged locomotive on Feltham's roster for virtually all of its BR existence was Class M7 0-4-4T No.30043 recorded on film on Thursday 25th August 1955. As LSWR No.43 the engine emerged from Nine Elms Works in March 1899, to work until withdrawn from 70B in May 1961. It was one of three M7 stationed at Feltham at that time, working from there on a few trip, shed pilot and yard shunting duties. Beyond, a good view is obtained of Feltham's ash crane and wagons, 50-gallon engine oil drums and scrap wood – for lighting-up – and behind all that, the depot's coaling tower with its four-section bunker, each with its own tippler, clearly visible. Note too, the asbestos shroud around the bunker top; this was applied in an attempt to stop flying coal dust! *C.W. Allen (ARPT)*

On Saturday 31st May 1958, a commendably clean Class S15, No.30513 (Eastleigh, March 1921), stands beside Feltham's high-roofed repair shop, wherein a 50-ton capacity overhead crane was installed, allowing heavy repairs to be undertaken. Designed by Mr Urie and introduced by the LSWR in 1920, for fast freight work, the S15 had many parts interchangeable with the Class N15 4-6-0 – the 'King Arthur' class – and twenty of the saturated boiler locomotives were in service at the Grouping. Mr Maunsell introduced some modifications, namely higher boiler pressure, superheating and slightly smaller diameter cylinders, which resulted in a measurable increase in performance, from which another forty-five of the class entered service in the years up to 1936. Eventually all the Urie engines were concentrated at Feltham from where they were very common sights around the west and north of London, on inter-Regional workings. The S15 was a genuine mixed-traffic engine and at times of heavy traffic, could be seen hauling passenger trains with considerable success. No.30513 is coupled to the Urie bogie tender of 5 tons coal and 5000 gallons of water capacity. Such equipped S15s were seen in the Western section of the Southern Railway and BR Southern Region, while those of the class working in the Central Section had, because of smaller turntable sizes, to be fitted with a 6-wheel, 4000 gallon tender. The pictured locomotive was withdrawn from Feltham in April 1963 but no fewer than seven S15 survive in preservation; two of Urie's design and five of Maunsell's. *C.J.B. Sanderson (ARPT)*

More than four years after the preceding picture – Sunday 23rd September 1962 – another locomotive posed beside 70B's repair shop. Probably the ugliest of British steam locomotives, the Class Q1, 0-6-0 was in fact, a very successful design, given the restraints in force when Mr Bulleid created it in 1942; while in service, the powerful machine proved formidable in its haulage capacity. With the need for new freight locomotives to handle WW2's enormous traffic, the SR draughtsmen had to make do with the minimum use of strategic materials and create a machine that would be light on maintenance. Borrowing from existing locomotive features – e.g. the firebox front and throat plates (copper in place of Bulleid's preferred steel), were taken from the 'Lord Nelson' 4-6-0 – and using new materials, like the first kind of fibreglass 'Idaglass,' for boiler cladding, 'Bulleid, Firth Brown' driving wheels and a smooth casing that could pass through washing plants, the Q1, though an Austerity design, served through until 1966, long after its first envisaged life span. The class totalled forty engines, of which Feltham depot maintained a stud through BR times that numbered between eight and twelve, and suddenly peaked at twenty-two by the beginning of 1962! Withdrawals started during 1963 with the featured locomotive, No.33013 (Brighton, October 1942), being taken out of service in July of that year. The doyen of the Q1 Class, No.33001, is preserved as part of the National Collection. *N.W. Skinner (ARPT)*

Wednesday 2nd January 1963 and Britain is in the grip of the fiercest winter for many years. So cold was it that fuel in diesel locomotives' tanks became too thick to be used, causing numerous steam locomotives, recently withdrawn, to be reinstated and carry the load, until winter retreated. The starkest of black and white contrasts are present in this picture of BR Standard Class 5 No.73114 of Nine Elms depot, standing at Feltham shed in the bitter cold. This particular locomotive was, of course, too young to have been one of those withdrawn and then resurrected for further service, having been delivered new from Doncaster Works, to 70A in October 1955. On 2nd April 1960, to maintain a Southern Railway tradition, No.73114 received the nameplates from withdrawn 'King Arthur' 4-6-0 No.30751 ETARRE. In fact other names from Arthurian legend would be bestowed upon all twenty Standard Class 5s allocated to the Southern Region at that time: 73080-73089 and 73110-73119. In the tales of that legend, Etarre was the love of one of Arthur's knights, Sir Pelleas – the *Gentle Knight* – but she would betray him with Arthur's nephew, Sir Gawain. 73114 would leave Nine Elms in August 1964, upon transfer to Eastleigh shed; it moved to Weymouth in October 1965 and would be taken out of use in June 1966. *A.Ives (ARPT)*

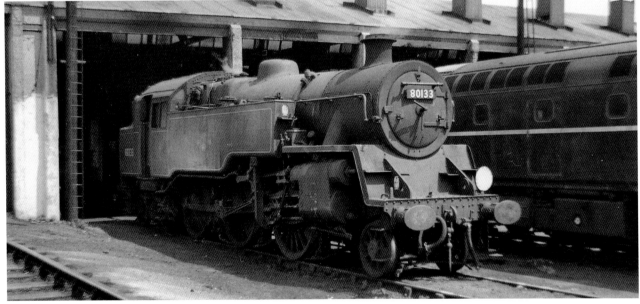

Standard steam locomotives did not come on to Feltham shed's books until the latter half of 1963 with the arrival of Class 5 4-6-0s and Class 4 2-6-4Ts plus a little later, Class 4 2-6-0s. Those types saw out the last months of Feltham shed before closure in July 1967. However, more than two years prior to that event, on Thursday 22nd April 1965, Standard Class 4 No.80133 (Brighton, March 1956), simmered in the Feltham sunshine alongside a BRCW Type 3 Bo-Bo diesel-electric. No.80133 carried no shedplate, but it was at the time allocated to 70A Nine Elms, from where it would be withdrawn at the end of steam on 9th July 1967. The locomotive had in fact been allocated to Feltham from August 1964, before it went to 70A, three months later. Prior to its arrival at Feltham the 2-6-4T had spent its short working life split between the London Tilbury & Southend lines and the Western Region's Swansea Division, lines. *John Reed (ARPT)*

In January 1963, historical records show the average low temperature around Feltham to have been -5 centigrade (!), so on Wednesday, the 2nd of that month, the driver of Class M7 0-4-4T No.30035 must have been very glad for his enclosed cab as he and his locomotive shunted wagons for the depot's coaling plant. The M7 had been built at Nine Elms works in April 1898 and the dawn of BR found her at Plymouth Friary shed. Leaving there in January 1960, No.30035 moved to Eastleigh and exactly a year later, to Feltham, where coal stage pilot and general shed duties would form the main employment. The 'Big Freeze' of January 1963 saved or deferred the fates of numerous steam locomotives around Britain, but not our subject here, which was withdrawn in February, that year. *A.Ives (ARPT)*

Nicknamed 'Black Motors' the Class 700 0-6-0s were common sights around the west of London hauling interchange traffic between Feltham and Brent Sidings. During summer 1958, the doyen of the class No.30687, is seen outside Feltham shed with Class O2 0-4-4T No.30179 looking on. Designed by Dugald Drummond, LSWR No.687 was built in March 1897 by Dübs & Co. (Maker's No.3510) at Queens Park Works, Glasgow. Initially an un-superheated design, the whole class was modified between 1922 and 1929 (687: June 1923) and even though superseded by Maunsell and Bulleid 0-6-0s and S15, 4-6-0 types, they continued to do useful work until the advent of the 1960s. No.30687 was a Feltham engine for all of its BR days, finally being withdrawn in September 1960. *K.H. Cockerill (ARPT)*

In April 1952, 'Greyhound' T9 No.30719 poses beside Feltham's repair shop. A number of things stand out: the engine is in lined black livery but has neither BR emblem nor wording on the tender side. Next, the T9's were allocated BR Power Classification 3P, which normally was painted on the cab side, near the engine number, but No.30719 has the letter H, which was a hangover from Urie's Southern Railway days of power classification. Lastly above the locomotive, the top level of the repair shop's windows are glazed – in other, later pictures (*see above*) it will be seen that those upper windows had been bricked-up. No.30719 was a Nine Elms engine, transferred there in April 1951 from Salisbury. It probably had hauled a local freight to Feltham yard, a typical duty for the locomotive (*see* section on Stewarts Lane, in Volume 2), and doubtless would return to Nine Elms Goods with a balancing working. Built by Dübs & Co. in September 1899 (Works No.3763), LSWR 719 had originally been paired with a 6-wheel tender, but this was replaced by an 8-wheel 'water cart' in November 1902. The engine was reallocated to Exmouth Junction in May 1959 and would be taken out of use in March 1961. *K.H.Cockerill (ARPT)*

Mention in the previous caption about Southern Railway power classifications being applied after Nationalisation – here is another example in this picture of O2 No.30230 at Feltham in April 1952. Instead of carrying classification 0P on the cabside, the 0-4-4T sports the letter K, from Urie's supposedly defunct scheme! Looking as if she had not long been out of a workshop overhaul, the O2 came to 70B in March 1952, from sleepy Dorchester, specifically to take over shed pilot duties and would continue in that vein until withdrawn in July 1956, five months short of a 62nd birthday. No.30230 was not immediately replaced; it would be four months before another of the type came to take up where 30230 had left off. *K.H.Cockerill (ARPT)*

SOUTHALL

Four separate sheds were sited at Southall. First, opened in 1859, was a one road building, probably in brick, for the Great Western & Brentford Railway, sited in the fork of the GWR's Down main line and the branch to Brentford; a turntable and coaling platform were provided outside the shed entrance. That depot was replaced on a site slightly further east, in 1884, by a brick built shed to the design of William Dean. It featured six through roads under a northlight roof, with a single road repair shed along the northern side. A new turntable and ramped coaling stage were provided, the latter under a water tank; at some later time a water softening plant was installed adjacent to the coaling stage's west end.

In 1904 a single road dead-end shed was provided alongside the Brentford branch for the steam rail-motors introduced to run passenger services over the branch. There matters rested until 1943 when following war damage, the six road shed's roof was replaced by a simple, almost flat design, with a large central smoke vent. By the beginning of the 1950s Southall's main building was in a parlous state so in a redevelopment between 1953 and 1955, the shed was completely demolished and replaced by a much larger structure. That comprised a six road through building in brick, steel and asbestos with a high, northlight roof and large circular smoke vents. A new repair shop was built in the rear yard, and a tub and hoist coaler appeared beside the shed; the original coal stage remained, supporting the water tank which had a new softening plant alongside. Lastly an adjoining two-road diesel shed was placed along the northern depot wall; the new roof covered that too. The rail-motor building was not affected by the project and remained standing until about 1960.

Coded variously by the GWR, 131 and SHL, BR Western Region allocated the code 81C, which the depot carried until closure to steam on 3rd January 1966. Diesels were stabled at the depot for a decade, then between 1993 and 1998 Southall shed was the base for the Paddington to Heathrow airport electrification scheme. Today it is home to several heritage locomotive preservation and operating groups.

The eastern end of Southall shed is seen during an enthusiast's society visit of Sunday 29th September 1957 when, as usual, many locomotives were 'on shed' being readied for the return to work next day. Three pannier tanks are identified: 5700 Class No.5727 (NBL 23845 [Queens Park Works], February 1929), which though a Southall locomotive for many years, would move in the next month to Cardiff Canton shed, where it would be withdrawn in May 1960. Behind 5727 is Southall's sole member of the Hawksworth 1500 Class pannier tanks, No.1501 (Swindon, July 1949), which had come to 81C from Old Oak Common in November 1950 and would remain until withdrawn in January 1961. Then, along with sisters Nos.1502 and 1509, it would go for further service with the National Coal Board. Later, all three were purchased by the Severn Valley Railway, with 1502 and 1509 being used for spares to restore 1501 to working order; still today, the locomotive is working on the SVR. Just peeping round the corner of 5727, another 5700 Class is noted – No.9789 (Swindon, May 1936), which would be a Western Region, London Division engine for its entire BR career, serving at different times, at 81A, 81B, 81C, 81D and 81F – not 81E Didcot – before being withdrawn from Oxford in December 1965. Of the recently rebuilt shed itself, the building at extreme right was the boiler house, while the northlight roofed extension behind 5727 was the repair shop associated with the diesel shed. *N.W.Skinner (ARPT)*

Southall – What was on shed Sunday 11th May 1952:
1462, 1474, 1501, 1605, 2285, 3618, 3620, 3704, 3750, 3799, 3816, 3862, 4608, 4610, 4673, 4695, 4944, 4956, 4996, 5401, 5410, 5414, 5415, 5727, 5755, 5799, 5918, 5989, 6110, 6125, 6128, 6147, 6937, 6942, 7315, 7730, 7731, 7732, 7910, 7918, 8752, 8753, 9300, 9301, 9316, 9407, 9641, 9726, 90152, 90207, 90268, 90355, 90484, 90697, W17   Total: 56.

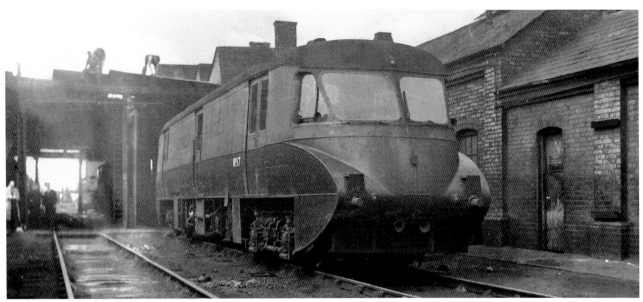

Southall was the base for two Great Western diesel railcars, which were interesting in that Nos.17 and 34 were introduced specifically for express parcels work from London, out to Reading and beyond (No.34 was more flexible in that it could haul trailing vehicles). In a less than perfect print, No.17 is seen at Southall on Sunday 27th August 1950, still in a grubby, GWR chocolate and cream livery. Built in 1936 by the Gloucester Railway Carriage and Wagon Company, with a carrying capacity of 10 tons, No.17 was powered by two AEC bus engines of 8.85 litres, delivering 130h.p. Each engine had its own 5-speed, pre-selector gearbox driving one bogie through a fluid coupling; maximum speed was 63 mph. As far as is known, railcar No.17 spent its working life based at Southall shed, being withdrawn in January 1959; not immediately disposed of, it was seen stored at Tyseley shed in March 1960. Of added interest, some work was in progress on Southall depot's emergency, flat roof, provided after 1943 wartime damage; almost certainly such 'patching' continued until commencement of the large scale rebuilding of the locomotive depot from 1953. *I.S. Jones (ARPT).*

Collett 0-4-2T No.1431 (Swindon, July 1934), receives a clean from its crew at Southall, sometime during 1959. Given the condition in which it was being kept, the locomotive was almost certainly one of the two engines of the type (at that time, No.1420 was the other 0-4-2T), which Southall maintained in good order for working the West Ealing–Greenford auto train. After leaving Swindon in 1934, No.1431 spent most of its working life in south and west Wales, before coming to Southall from Goodwick, in April 1958, when many London-based enthusiasts were very pleased with the reallocation of such an obscure engine! The 0-4-2T did not stay long though, being moved to Gloucester, in January 1960, to undergo withdrawal in April 1961 from Gloucester's sub-shed at Lydney. *A.R.Thompson (ARPT)*

BR Standard 9F 2-10-0 No.92244 seems not to be in steam as it resides in Southall shed at 10.20 am on a dull day, the exact date of which was not recorded. However, the locomotive, which some wag has crudely christened *The Flyer,* carries an Old Oak Common shed plate. The 9F was allocated to 81A between November 1958 and October 1960, so this picture comes from that period and given that the Standard was new (Crewe, November 1958) when it went to 81A and looking at its condition in the photograph, it was probably towards the end of its sojourn at Old Oak. No.92244 would move on from 81A in October 1960, to spend time at a number of south Wales depots before ending its days at Gloucester, from where it was withdrawn in January 1966, just eight years old. *Norman Preedy.*

It is almost 4.15 pm on the afternoon of Sunday 29th July 1962, yet another gloomy British summer day! The doyen of Class 4700, is quietly simmering while waiting for its next duty – a fast freight no doubt, but to where? Bristol, or Plymouth, or Wolverhampton – they all were regular destinations for this class of just nine machines, the last design of Mr Churchward, specifically for fast overnight freight haulage. No.4700 itself left Swindon Works in May 1919, being first allocated to St Philips Marsh shed in Bristol and by the beginning of the BR era it was based at Old Oak Common. The 2-8-0 moved from Old Oak to Southall in June 1961 but would be withdrawn just three months after this picture was taken. The pannier tank seen at left was 5700 Class No.3620 (Swindon, May 1939), a long-term resident of 81C from where it was withdrawn in June 1965. *Norman Preedy.*

So, now and then the sun *does* smile on Southall shed! Well, at least it was shining at 3.40 pm on the afternoon of Sunday 4th October 1959 to nicely illuminate Class 2884 No.3801 from Severn Tunnel Junction depot. Doubtless the next day the 2-8-0 would return to its Monmouthshire home with a sizeable train – just what the type was intended for and though basically a somewhat dated design, these locomotives were most capable machines with a standard maximum load of 100 wagons! In fact so well thought of were the 2800 and 2884 classes that no fewer than sixteen survive in preservation – seven of Class 2800 and nine of Class 2884. However, 3801 was not one of those; emerging from Swindon works in December 1938 it seems to have spent its working life based in South Wales, ending its days at shed 86E, until withdrawal in August 1964. *N.W.Skinner (ARPT).*

Seen at the same time as No.3801 in the preceding picture, Class 4700, 2-8-0 No.4703 (Swindon, March 1922), also basks in the sunshine, having it seems, recently hauled a train with reporting number 162 – see the faint remains of that number on the smokebox door. Based at St. Philips Marsh depot, the mixed traffic 2-8-0 looks quite spruce and soon – probably that night – would make its way west, back to Bristol with a fast freight. No.4703 would actually move to Southall from 82B, in September 1962, then on to Old Oak Common two months later. The 2-8-0 would be withdrawn from 81A in May 1964, along with sisters 4705 and 4707, thereby rendering this impressive locomotive type extinct. Today, however, the 4709 Project is making good progress with the building of a replica Class 4700 from a mixture of parts donated by other withdrawn locomotives that were beyond economic restoration, plus some very costly new build items. But, such is the enthusiasm for seeing a 4700 back on the rails the project seems assured of success. Of additional notice, see the Pannier tank on the right of 4703; note the standard method of hanging fire-irons, shovels, and buckets from the bunker lamp brackets. *N.W.Skinner (ARPT).*

This picture of a locomotive seen at Southall, missing a number plate, is so typical of what the end of steam brought about, and is especially saddening for your scribe who has to confess that GWR 'Castles' have always been his favourite type of steam locomotive. No.4089 was part of the second batch of ten 'Castles' built, being completed at Swindon in July 1925 and named for a fortress at Donnington, near Newbury founded in 1386. Built by Sir Richard Abberbury it is said the castle saw visits from Henry VIII and Elizabeth I and later withstood an eighteen month siege by Parliamentary forces during

the English Civil War. Parliament ordered the castle's destruction in 1646 but a twin-towered gatehouse still stands, in the care of English Heritage. The locomotive DONNINGTON CASTLE was not nearly so long-lived. Seen on Sunday 30th August 1964, it looks careworn and indeed – after 39 years' service – would be withdrawn during the following month from its then home depot at Reading. *J.Archer (ARPT)*

After the sadness generated by the previous picture, this self-confessed devotee of the GWR 'Castles' has included this portrait as a morale- restorer. A magnificent engine carrying a magnificent name, but *still* there is sadness! No.5017 is seen beside Southall shed on Sunday 9th September 1962, just twelve days before the locomotive was withdrawn from service at her home shed at Horton Road, Gloucester. It would remain in store at Gloucester until 14th November when it was moved to Cashmore's, Newport, where within a month it had been dismantled. Why do away with a machine that looks at least, to be in fine fettle? Simple – the rapid adoption of diesel power rendered our subject and many of her sisters, and of many other classes, redundant; there was no need to retain them in working order and costing British Railways to keep them so. Emerging from Swindon Works in July 1932 as ST. DONAT'S CASTLE, it was named for a fortress near Cardiff built circa 1300, with additions in the 14th and 15th centuries, and still standing, in use as a college. No.5017 would be renamed in April 1954 to THE GLOUCESTERSHIRE REGIMENT, 28TH, 61ST. The renaming honoured the men of that regiment for their epic and self-sacrificing stand, as part of a United Nations force, against the Communist Chinese, at the Battle of Imjin River, Korea, from Sunday 22nd to Wednesday 25th April 1951. During thirty years and two months service, No.5017 amassed very nearly 1.6 million miles, or just over 53,000 miles per year, statistics which prompt an associated musing: how much was that in terms of the total amounts of tons of coal and gallons of water, consumed? *Howard Forster.*

More despondency from the last months of steam at Southall – and another fittingly grey day, Sunday 23rd October 1965! Perhaps pondering their futures, which would not be long, a pair of ill-cared for 6100 class 2-6-2 tanks simmer quietly in the yard. At left is No.6165 (Swindon, October 1935), minus both the smokebox number and shed plate. The locomotive had been a Southall engine since moving from Old Oak Common in August 1964 and despite formally being reallocated to Worcester, during October 1965, with just a week remaining it obviously had been reluctant to make the move! But go to Worcester it did, to be withdrawn at the end of December 1965, being noted there, in store in January 1966. No.6145 (Swindon, December 1932), at least had kept its smokebox number plate, but the shed plate is again missing. However, some attempt had been made with a chalked-on oval shape and the engine's depot code, 81F Oxford, where it had been resident since June 1965. Like her sister, 6145 would be withdrawn at the end December that year, with the demise of steam on BR's Western Region. *Geoff Kent.*

Ex-LNER Class A4 No.60007 SIR NIGEL GRESLEY (Doncaster, November 1937) visited Paddington station on Saturday 23rd October 1965. The locomotive worked through from Manchester (Exchange), via Birmingham, hauling the light load of five coaches, of train 1X36, *THE PADDINGTON STREAMLINER* rail tour, which was run with the specific purpose of generating funds for the purchase of the locomotive for future generations. Old Oak Common depot had recently closed to steam, so No.60007 went to Southall for servicing before it returned from Paddington, whence it came, and it is seen here being refuelled by 81C's rudimentary coaler. That the A4 was saved for posterity needs no further telling, so thankfully it may still be seen in operation today – sometimes, but not often enough, on the main line. *Geoff Kent.*

A nice trio of Southall engines, seen 'on-shed' on Sunday 19th April 1953. At left is 5400 Class No.5415, built at Swindon in May 1932 for branch line and mainline stopping passenger trains, for which latter duty, it was fitted with 5ft 2in. wheels. A lifetime resident of Southall the 0-6-0PT would be withdrawn in September 1957. Next is 2884 Class No.3845, a wartime product from Swindon being put into traffic during April 1942; the 2-8-0 had just arrived at Southall, on transfer from Didcot and in May 1955 would move to Oxley, then South Wales, before going to Banbury to finish its days, in June 1964. The last locomotive, 'Hall' No.5953 DUNLEY HALL, was built in December 1935 and had come to 81C two months before this picture was recorded, from Ebbw Junction shed. In November 1957, the engine would move to Llanelly and remain in West Wales until a final move to St. Philips Marsh in February 1961; it was withdrawn from the Bristol shed in October 1962. Dunley Hall, near Stourport, Worcestershire, exists today, a 450 years old Grade II Listed structure in use as a care home! As with a number of instances of Great Western 4-6-0s, mostly named for buildings, there was a 'Manor' No.7811 DUNLEY MANOR, but that was named for a different building, near Litchfield, Hampshire, still used as a private residence. *Norman Preedy.*

2884 Class No.3812 gently simmers at Southall shed on Saturday 22nd May 1965. It carries an 86A shed plate, denoting Newport Ebbw Junction depot, but in fact the engine had been transferred from there to 81C in March 1965; once again though, the shed plate had not been changed. Nor would it be most likely, as the very tired looking 2-8-0 would be withdrawn during the following month of June. *K. Groundwater (ARPT)*

OLD OAK COMMON

This was the largest engine shed operated by the GWR, with four turntables under a single, Churchward design gabled roof; it provided a model for further turntable, and also, straight sheds of all sizes, going forward to the end of the 1920s. Old Oak Common opened in March 1906, replacing two cramped buildings of 1855 and 1862, sited at Westbourne Park, that depot having superseded the original combined roundhouse and straight shed provided in 1838 with the first Paddington station.

Coded 101, then PDN, Old Oak depot included a large workshop where major repairs could be undertaken, and a double-sided ramped coaling stage supporting a massive water tank of 290,000 gallons capacity. Destined to house locomotives for working express and local passenger services from and to London, together with a myriad of carriage stock movements, plus some local freight turns and yard shunters, Old Oak was the atypical 'cathedral of steam,' never failing to impress visitors with vistas of its huge allocation of locomotives – 232 were on the depot's roster on 31st December 1947, the last day of the GWR. That figure included the following 4-6-0s: thirty-three 'Castles'; nine 'Kings'; eight 'Counties'; thirty-seven 'Halls' and two 'Granges'. Unsurprisingly the depot was frequently short of stabling room so in the early 1950s a carriage shed was built just to the south-west corner of the main building and it saw almost continuous, partial use for holding locomotives – mostly those deemed spare to requirements and stored, or 'stopped' for some other reason. British Railways allocated the shed code 81A which was carried through to the end of WR steam on 22nd March 1965, following which diesels used the depot. For the diesels the place was reduced to a single open turntable, with the repair shop retained, until final closure in 2009. As these words are written (late-2016), the site of Old Oak Common is under development for an electric multiple unit depot and other buildings, associated with London's Crossrail Project.

Old Oak was such a massive place that it was well-nigh impossible to get a complete panorama of the exterior. Probably the best vantage point was from the south-east corner of the shed yard, as here on Sunday 15th March 1959. The large, double-sided coaling plant obscures three of the six gabled roofs covering the four internal turntables, but above the Pannier tank at right, a small portion of the repair shop's high roof is visible; in the far distance, are the twin chimneys of Acton Lane power station. That Pannier is No.3688, which went new, to Old Oak in January 1941, staying until reallocation to Duffryn Yard, in January 1961, from where it was withdrawn on September 1962. The only other identifiable locomotive is condensing Pannier No.9707, which emerged from Swindon in December 1933 to spend most of its working life at Old Oak until transferring to Southall in November 1963 from where it was officially transferred in August 1964 to Taunton. That was an incongruous shift for a locomotive specifically built for London services so unsurprisingly the transfer never took place and 9707 was withdrawn just one month later. Two other points of note are the raised jib of the bucket crane that was almost continuously in action, clearing ash from the pits around the water tank area, and the locomotive seen in steam in the left distance. That was the usual place for stabling Old Oak's standby engine, or engines, which almost always were members of the shed's stud of 'Castle' class machines. *Norman Preedy.*

Old Oak Common – What was on shed Wednesday 16th April 1952:
1008, 1026, 2276, 2846, 3017, 3648, 3688, 3715, 3854, 4032, 4048, 4644, 4698, 4699, 4702, 4705, 4707, 4708, 4929, 4941, 5000, 5012, 5020, 5040, 5055, 5056, 5069, 5081, 5087, 5092, 5717, 5931, 5937, 5939, 5945, 5947, 5960, 5996, 6001, 6120, 6142, 6144, 6149, 6155, 6168, 6368, 6821, 6865, 6927, 6944, 6951, 6957, 6960, 6983, 6996, 7001, 7004, 7027, 7032, 7033, 7902, 7904, 7914, 8764, 8767, 8769, 8770, 8772, 9411, 9423, 9725, 9751, 70020, 70023, 90069, 15105, 15203, 18000   Total: 78.

Old Oak Common was famous for the numerous photographs taken inside, where the many locomotives ranged around the four turntables presented an inspiring sight! Here, from early 1950, in one corner of the vast building, one can get a good idea of how the high gabled, Churchward roof was built, with much cross-bracing and suspended gas pipes etc., among the smoke vents; see too, the standpipe for hot water washing-out. Two of 81A's resident engines are seen: 2251 Class No.2282, still with buffer beam number, but carrying a BR shed plate, was under light repair. Built in January 1936 the locomotive first went to Didcot shed but

by Nationalisation it was based at Old Oak. In time it would move to Goodwick, from where it was withdrawn in May 1960. The other locomotive, bearing a NOT TO BE MOVED plate, is most worthy of remark. 'Castle' No.4016 SOMERSET LIGHT INFANTRY (PRINCE ALBERT'S) (SLI) started life in April 1908 as 'Star' No.4016 KNIGHT OF THE GOLDEN FLEECE, being rebuilt to a 'Castle' in October 1925, carrying the same name, until it was renamed SLI in January 1938. Going new in 1908, to Old Oak Common, the engine finished its days at the same depot, from where it was withdrawn in September 1951, after 43 years' service. The SLI regiment had its origins in Jacobite days and went through many re-namings and re-arrangement of names, before finally becoming the Somerset Light Infantry (Prince Albert's) in January 1921. The SLI merged with the Duke of Cornwall's Light Infantry in 1959 and was further merged nine years later with the three other regiments in the Light Infantry Brigade to form The Light Infantry. Today even that title has gone, with all that vast military history and tradition now coming under the title The Rifles. *S.C. Crook (ARPT).*

Outside Old Oak's large repair shop about May 1956, a trio of locomotives wait their turn to move, via the traverser into the next free repair bay. 'King' No.6016 KING EDWARD V was based at 81A at the time, having transferred from Wolverhampton (Stafford Road) in December 1954. The engine would be fitted with a double chimney in January 1958 and at the end of the same year, move to Plymouth (Laira), leaving there in June 1962 to go back to Stafford Road, from where it was withdrawn three months later. Edward V of England never was formally crowned King. Born on 2nd November 1470, he succeeded to the Crown upon his father, Edward IV's death on 9th April 1483. He was housed in the Tower of London with his younger brother Richard, but both disappeared on 26th June 1483, not to again be seen – whether murdered or not has never fully been established. Edward V was succeeded by his uncle, who became Richard III. The 7200 class 2-8-2 tank engines were more usually associated with South Wales, but No.7239 spent the period June 1953 to September 1962, at Oxford from which shed it was visiting Old Oak for a repair job too big for its home depot to deal with. Built in February 1936, No.7239 spent time at, among other places, Banbury and Severn Tunnel Junction, before moving to Oxford. The engine would finish its days in October 1963, working from Llanelly depot. *K.C.H. Cockerill (ARPT)*

The words Grace and Symmetry come to mind when one looks upon a 'Star' class 4-6-0; pure Edwardian elegance! No.4056 PRINCESS MARGARET was visiting Old Oak in the autumn of 1953, from its home shed of Bristol, Bath Road. Sadly not as clean as she could be, No.4056 was built in July 1914, going first to Old Oak Common. But by the beginning of BR the engine was associated with Bristol and in this picture has been turned and coaled, ready for the return journey to its home from where it would continue to work until being withdrawn in October 1957, the last of her illustrious type. Note the elbow steam pipes, fitted to the 4-6-0 in 1949 and a feature of a number of her sisters, along with 'Castle' type pipes – or, no pipes at all, as built. The locomotive was named for Princes Margaret of Connaught (1882 – 1920), a granddaughter of Queen Victoria, who became Crown Princess of Sweden. *S.C. Crook (ARPT)*.

An enthusiast inspects what, by May 1953, would have been a rare sight at Old Oak Common – a GWR outside-framed 4-4-0. It was Sunday 31st May when 'Dukedog' No.9028 was visiting from its then home shed of Oxford and the engine had a complex history! Completed in November 1939 as No.3228, it was comprised of boiler and frames of earlier, withdrawn 4-4-0 locomotives. The boiler came from 'Duke' No.3256 which had emerged from Swindon in August 1895, as No.3255 (note the different number, later renumbered) EXCALIBUR; that engine was withdrawn in June 1936. The frames of No.9028 came from 'Bulldog' Class, No.3429, which was built at Swindon in July 1906, as No.3719 (later renumbered), never carried a name and was withdrawn in August 1939. Renumbered from 3228 to 9028 in 1946, the 'Dukedog' served all its time on the Cambrian section, between Oswestry and Machynlleth, before being moved to 81F in November 1952. Its residency at Oxford was brief though, with a final move to 84J Croes Newydd in June 1953, from where it was taken out of service in September 1957. *C.W.Allen (ARPT.*

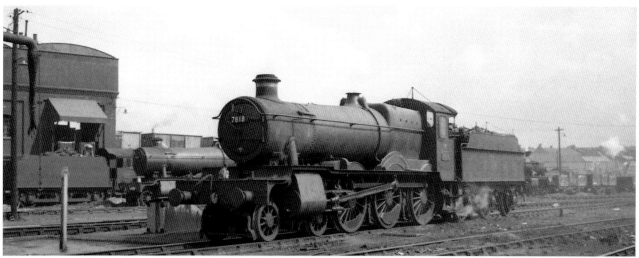

With the exception of a few short periods of allocation to Reading, Manor class 4-6-0s were rarely seen in the Western Region's London Division and then usually on running-in turns after major repairs at Swindon. So the appearance at 81A, of No.7818 GRANVILLE MANOR on Wednesday 29th August 1956, was an event worthy of photographing, especially as the tender still carried GWR on the flanks! No.7818 was based at Tyseley at the time but what brought it to London may only be speculated upon; doubtless it soon returned to its Birmingham home. The 'Manor' would later move to Newton Abbot, then Machynlleth, before returning to Tyseley in November 1962, from where it was withdrawn in January 1965. The building for which the locomotive was named still exists, though much modified, in Bideford, Devon and dates back to the de Grenville family of Normandy, which later changed its name to Granville. *Howard Foster.*

Fifteen 'Britannia' Pacifics were allocated to the Western Region from new, divided between Old Oak Common, Laira Plymouth and Cardiff Canton sheds. It is common lore that the locomotive men at Old Oak and Laira did not like the BR 4-6-2s, due no doubt to traditional conservatism, but also the important fact that Western locomotives and signalling were set up for right-hand drive from the footplate, whereas the Britannia's were left hand drive. Cardiff Canton men, however, were quite happy with the engines so it can be no surprise that by December 1956 all

the Region's Britannia's were concentrated at 86C. Here we see No.70019 LIGHTNING, one of the Class 7 Pacifics then allocated to 83D, stopped for some reason and parked outside the 1950s carriage shed at Old Oak, doubtless waiting attention. The date was Sunday 4th September 1955, but how long the Pacific remained at 81A is unknown. Eventually the locomotive joined its sisters in leaving the Western Region in two batches, June 1958 and September 1961, for the London Midland Region. No.70019 would be based at six different LM Region depots before it was withdrawn at Upperby in March 1966. *Clive Allen (ARPT).*

Old Oak Common – Sunday 29th August 1954:
1005, 1503, 1505, 2252, 2276, 2282, 2808, 2895, 3023, 3217, 3754, 3808, 3825, 3829, 3831, 3839, 3840, 4078, 4080, 4082, 4089, 4615, 4644, 4704, 4705, 4708, 4921, 4939, 4963, 4979, 5021, 5027, 5028, 5051, 5055, 5063, 5066, 5081, 5093, 5095, 5918, 5939, 5940, 5989, 6000, 6007, 6012, 6015, 6019, 6020, 6021, 6024, 6109, 6110, 6120, 6121, 6129, 6137, 6141, 6142, 6149, 6155, 6159, 6168, 6325, 6834, 6853, 6854, 6875, 6877, 6920, 6929, 6954, 6959, 6961, 6962, 6974, 6987, 6990, 7001, 7013, 7025, 7033, 7036, 7791, 7902, 7904, 7905, 8432, 8707, 8751, 8756, 8757, 8760, 8765, 8768, 8772, 9318, 9412, 9422, 9423, 9700, 9701, 9702, 9704, 9705, 9708, 9709, 9710, 9751, 9754, 70015, 70018, 70023, 70026, 75003, 13031, 13032, 13033, 15105   Total: 120.

This photograph of No.6011 KING JAMES I, leaving the south-east turntable is dated 5th May 1956 – FA Cup Final day at Wembley stadium, when Birmingham City met Manchester City. The locomotive was based at Wolverhampton Stafford Road at the time and it is well known that Wolverhampton Wanderers football supporters did not like *any* Birmingham team at all! So it seems likely that some wag at 84A had chalked 'BRUM 0 – MANCHESTER CITY 5' on the smoke box, to irritate the Birmingham supporters that doubtless were hauled by the 'King' from Birmingham to London that day! As it transpired, Manchester City won 2-0, so No.6011's journey back was probably with a train load of very glum Birmingham fans. No.6011 was built in April 1928, was fitted with a double chimney in March 1956 and spent all its BR years at Wolverhampton until September 1962 when it moved to Old Oak, to be withdrawn three months later, having amassed over 1.7 million miles since entering service. King James the First of England was born 19th June 1566, the son of Mary, Queen of Scots, becoming the infant King James VI of Scotland on 24th July 1567. Following the union of the English and Scottish Crowns on 24th March 1603, he became King James I of England and Ireland. He died on 27th March 1625, to be succeeded by Charles I. *Norman Preedy.*

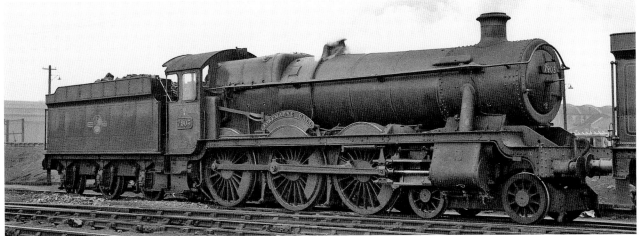

Old Oak Common's resident 'Modified Hall' (Class 6959) No.7903 FORMARKE HALL, rests on the coaling road, on Saturday 17th May 1958. Built in April 1949 the 4-6-0 went new to Old Oak where it remained until October 1963, when it transferred to Cardiff, East Dock from where it was withdrawn in June 1964. Sent to Woodham's scrapyard at Barry, the locomotive survived to be purchased for preservation and it can be seen today, operating on the Gloucestershire and Warwickshire Railway. Your scribe has a particular memory of this engine as on Sunday 21st October 1956, it hauled a train carrying among the passengers, the Home Counties Locospotters' Club from Paddington to Newport. Much remembered is the sparkling performance, including a speed in the high 80s in the bottom depths of the Severn Tunnel, and a footplate overflowing with youthful enthusiasm when the friendly crew let many of us into the cab at Newport. Sheds visited in what was basically a half-day were 86A, 86B, 86C, 88A and 88B, with hundreds of locomotives copped! The return from Cardiff to London was behind Old Oak 'Castle' No.5044 EARL OF DUNRAVEN, with the train carrying many naval reservists who had been attending Trafalgar Day celebrations – such are memories! Completed in 1762 as the ancestral home of the Burdett family, Foremarke Hall is situated near the village of Repton, South Derbyshire. The Grade 1 listed structure is today used as a preparatory school. *C.J.B. Sanderson (ARPT)*

A PLETHORA OF PANNIERS! Old Oak Common was known for its large fleet of Pannier tanks, many of which could be seen at all times, lined-up in the yard, especially the area around the coaling stage; relatively few were routinely housed inside the four-turntable shed. Here is a small sample:

Showing one or two scrapes and 'dimples' in its side tanks, 5700 class No.5775 sits beside Old Oak's coaling stage on Monday 24th June 1963. Built in September 1929 the Pannier spent all its working life, up to an official withdrawal date of July 1963, based at depots in South Wales, so what was it doing at Old Oak so near the apparent end of its life? Simple – it was not near its life's end, but sporting a nicely cleaned exterior, for delivery to London Transport (LT) at its Neasden depot, where it would become L89. Serving with LT until 1969 the locomotive was purchased in January 1970 by the Keighley & Worth Valley Railway (KWVR), where it immediately had a part in the film version of *The Railway Children*. Today it is out of service, waiting considerable repairs by the KWVR to restore it to working order. *F.W. Hampson (ARPT)*

Dwarfed by Old Oak's large, high-roofed repair shop, Pannier No.8759 simmers away on Sunday 10th January 1960. The engine has the design of cab introduced in 1933 with engine No.8750; officially still classed as 5700, such modified locomotives were unofficially known as the 8750 Class. No.8759 itself came out of Swindon Works in October 1933 and spent its entire working life at Old Oak, until withdrawal in January 1963. At right is sister No.8772, another long-term resident of the shed, from building in January 1934 until moved to Duffryn Yard shed in August 1960, where it was condemned exactly one year later. *C.J.B. Sanderson (ARPT).*

The GWR handled much meat traffic, which had to be worked over the Metropolitan Railway's underground route between Paddington and Smithfield Market. Accordingly in 1932, Pannier No.8700 was modified by fitting condensing gear together with a Weir recirculating pump and trialled for a year. The locomotive was a great success so it was renumbered 9700 (a new 8700 was built in 1934), and ten more of the type constructed between September and December 1933. They were stationed at Old Oak for all their lives (except 9707 – *see* Old Oak image and caption above), and withdrawn between January 1959 (9708) and November 1964 (9706). Because of their rather sedentary lives it seems the 97xx class were not frequent visitors to Swindon for overhaul. This is evidenced from the two pictures illustrated: at right, No.9710 is seen inside 81A's southwest shed on Saturday 17th May 1958. Note the locomotive still carried the GWR roundel signage, ten years after the GWR ceased to exist – so no visit to works in BR times? The Weir pump is just visible at left with one of the two recirculating pipes to the side tanks which were extended giving a capacity of 1250 gallons, rendering the 97xx a sort of hybrid Pannier/Side tank locomotive. *C.J.B. Sanderson (ARPT)*

In this image it seems 9709 had not visited works since GWR days as it sits on Old Oak's 'condemned' line on Thursday 16th August 1962. Withdrawn in May of that year, the Pannier still carried GWR on the tank sides, fourteen years on. 'Castle' No.5082 SWORDFISH, withdrawn from 81A in July 1962, also awaits the call to the breaker's yard. Built in June 1939, named POWIS CASTLE, the engine was renamed in January 1941, to pay tribute to the Royal Navy's venerable Fairey Swordfish torpedo bomber. *David J. Dippie.*

When Hawksworth became Locomotive Engineer to the GWR, he saw no immediate reason to move away from the general layout and dimensions of the 5700 class Pannier tanks, but produced further examples of the basic engine with his own 'look' which gave the appearance of a chunkier, more powerful machine. The 9400 class started with a batch of ten in 1947 then British Railways, Western Region, decided upon extending the fleet with a second batch of ninety engines, to be built by Robert Stephenson & Hawthorns Co., with the first being delivered in February 1950. (A third batch, of a further one-hundred locomotives, was later delivered – fifty each – by Messrs Bagnall and the Yorkshire Engine Company). Here is the first RSH-built engine, No.9410, at Old Oak Common on Thursday 16th August 1962, having been withdrawn in the previous month after an operational life of just twelve years and five months! The 0-6-0PT had gone new to Barry and then found its way via Reading, to 81A, arriving in May 1951. *David J. Dippie.*

Hawksworth's last design for the GWR was another type of Pannier tank, and this time there were radical differences, although the basic dimensions and power were the same as the 5700 and 9400 types. Where the 1500 Class differed is that it utilised outside, Walschaerts valve gear, had no running plate and incorporated much welded, instead of riveted construction. Only ten were built, by BR during 1949, the first six going to Old Oak, the other four, initially to Newport Pill shed, for dock shunting. Those based at 81A were mainly used for working empty stock between Old Oak carriage sidings and Paddington station and your scribe will never forget the sound the 1500s made as they rushed the bank

out of the sidings up to the Ladbroke Grove flyover – it was inspiring stuff! On Sunday 3rd June 1962, No.1506 was on the coaling road at Old Oak. It had been allocated to 81A in the previous month, from Newport Ebbw Junction shed and would reside until withdrawal in December 1963, along with three sisters, rendering the type extinct on BR. Happily though, as related in the earlier section on Southall depot, No.1501 has been preserved. *N.W. Skinner (ARPT).*

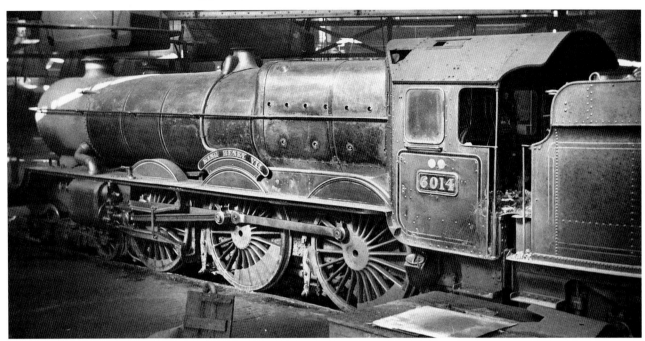

These images illustrate two factors that applied to the King class, the second in fact, a feature of just one member of the class. At top we see Laira, Plymouth's No.6014 KING HENRY VII, inside Old Oak in the spring of 1953. The locomotive still carries the blue livery in which all Kings were painted in the first days of BR. However, the poor condition of the paintwork is a very graphic demonstration of its low performance in everyday use, which is why it was not continued for any of the locomotives given the livery, throughout BR. Next, this particular engine was built in May 1928 and seven years later became, with 'Castle' No.5005 MANORBIER CASTLE, the subject of the Great Western's experiment to come into the 'streamliner' age, following the mechanical and publicity success of Gresley's A4 Pacifics. Unfortunately the GW's attempt was nothing short of lamentably and amateurishly ugly and all but one trace of the streamlining had been removed from No.6014 by 1943. What remained was the wedge-shaped cab front, clearly seen in the photograph. The 4-6-0 was fitted with a double chimney in September 1957 and the second illustration reveals this and the retained wedge cab front, during the engine's visit to Old Oak on Sunday 11th October 1959. By then KING HENRY VII had been transferred to Stafford Road, where it would remain until withdrawal in September 1962, with 1.83 million miles 'on the clock.' The last British king to win the crown on the field of battle, Henry VII seized the throne after defeating Richard III at the Battle of Bosworth and established the House of Tudor royal line. Born on 28th January 1457, Harry Tudor also ruled the Principality of Wales (until 29th November 1489), and was Lord of Ireland, until his death on 21st April 1509, when he was succeeded by Henry VIII. *S.C. Crook and N.W. Skinner (ARPT).*

Due homage is being paid at Old Oak Common in March 1959! On standby duty, 'Castle' No.7017 carries the illustrious name of G.J.CHURCHWARD, the Great Western's innovative genius of a Chief Mechanical Engineer (1902-1922). Built in August 1948, the locomotive went first to Old Oak and soon after to Cardiff Canton depot. It transferred back to 81A in August 1954, remaining at the shed until being withdrawn in August 1963 at the disgracefully premature age of 15 years. Sadly the locomotive was not preserved, but the name of George Jackson Churchward lives on in railway folklore. *Norman Preedy.*

Forever considering itself different from the other British railway companies, the GWR always sought innovation. One attempt to find a replacement for steam traction was to use gas turbine driven locomotives, two of which were ordered in 1946, to be delivered in 1950. The first, numbered 18000 came from Brown-Boveri of Switzerland, the second, 18100, from Metropolitan Vickers; they were rated at 2500 and 3000 horsepower, respectively. Nicknamed the 'Kerosene Castles' that appellation was not appropriate for 18000 which burned heavy bunker oil while 18100 used kerosene. No matter what fuel used the locomotives were not a success because at sea level, gas turbines have to operate at near maximum output and this resulted in horrendous fuel consumption at a time when 'Austerity Britain' was trying to keep down such costs. So the engines were taken out of service after a few years and had varied subsequent histories. No.18100 was modified into an a.c. electric locomotive and went on to help BR set up Britain's first 25Kv electrified main line; after which it was left to rot and was eventually broken up. No.18000 survived without its working innards and appropriately its empty shell may today be found at the Great Western Society's museum at Didcot. The picture dates from a gloomy Tuesday 14th April 1957, with 18000 once again receiving attention outside Old Oak's repair shop; it still carries the head code of its last working: No.470, the 2.15 pm Bristol – Paddington semi-fast passenger train. If a steam locomotive could smirk, no doubt 81A's No.5014 GOODRICH CASTLE would be grinning at its supposed replacement's discomfiture! *F.W. Hampson (ARPT)*

Old Oak Common – What was on shed Sunday 25th February 1962:
1006, 1500, 1503, 1504, 1507, 3646, 3750, 3754, 3805, 4082, 4085, 4700, 4701, 4917, 4951, 4986, 5002, 5011, 5015, 5057, 5060, 5066, 5080, 5084, 5093, 5932, 5933, 5966, 5973, 6002, 6003, 6015, 6016, 6022, 6023, 6025, 6026, 6027, 6135, 6142, 6163, 6164, 6168, 6169, 6857, 6924, 6954, 6955, 6956, 6959, 7010, 7018, 7020, 7021, 7028, 7029, 7030, 7921, 8435, 8458, 8459, 8756, 8757, 8759, 8761, 8763, 8767, 8771, 8773, 9405, 9418, 9419, 9420, 9423, 9450, 9469, 9479, 9658, 9659, 9661, 9702, 9707, 9709, 9725, 9784, 48412, 90485, 90563, 92204, 92217, 92226, D601, D801, D845, D869, D870, D3031, D3032, D3033, D3114, D3406, D3598, D3600, D3602, D3604, D3947, D3954, D3962, D4000, D4003, D4004, D4006, D7003   Total: 113.

No.6024 KING EDWARD I transferred to Old Oak in September 1954 after spending many years at Plymouth Laira shed. Built in June 1930 the 4-6-0 was fitted with a double chimney in March 1957 and in that modified condition it is seen on Tuesday 23rd August 1960, backing off Old Oak depot to pick up its train at Paddington. No.6024 was reallocated from 81A in September 1961, to Cardiff Canton, where it worked out its last months to withdrawal in June 1962. Luckily the engine went to Woodham's scrapyard, Barry, from where it was purchased for preservation in 1973. It later ran on the main lines of Britain for many years before passing into the care of the Royal Scot Locomotive and General Trust which is chaired by millionaire railway enthusiast Jeremy Hosking. Currently (January 2017) No.6024 is undergoing a heavy repair so that it may return to main line working. Of interest is the youthful trainspotter. The area around Old Oak Common in northwest London saw a large influx of people from the West Indies in the early 1950s, primarily for employment by London Transport. No matter what a person's origins, it is evident that the steam locomotive held an eternal fascination; let us hope the young chap copped 6024 that day! Edward I (18th June 1239 – 7th July 1307) succeeded his father, Henry III on 12th November 1272, but was not crowned until his return to England from the ninth Crusade in 1274. Known as 'longshanks' because of his height and also 'Hammer of the Scots,' Edward I was also involved in crushing rebellions among the Welsh. Upon his death he was succeeded by his son, Edward II. *David J. Dippie.*

On the first day of BR there were two 'Grange' class 4-6-0s allocated to Old Oak Common: No.6865 HOPTON GRANGE and No.6869 RESOLVEN GRANGE. They soon moved away and for the remainder of the steam era at 81A, no other 'Grange' was allocated to the shed; which always made the sight of a 68xx something exciting, like here on Saturday 17th May 1958, when No.6820 KINGSTONE GRANGE, was paying a visit from its home shed at Worcester. No.6820 would eventually transfer to Newport Ebbw Junction, then Cardiff East Dock, from where it was withdrawn in July 1965.

The building for which the engine was named is a circa 1600, large farmhouse at Kingstone, Herefordshire. Today it is a Grade II Listed structure in the care of English Heritage. *C.J.B. Sanderson (ARPT)*

Old Oak Common – What was on shed Sunday 28th April 1963:

3711, 3750, 3754, 4087, 4615, 4910, 4929, 4972, 5014, 5041, 5065, 5070, 5919, 6005, 6010, 6020, 6913, 7017, 7027, 7037, 8420, 8458, 8487, 8756, 8757, 8763, 8765, 9405, 9419, 9423, 9455, 9479, 9495, 9659, 9661, 9710, 9784, D806, D809, D827, D839, D846, D865, D1002, D1011, D1013, D1014, D1035, D1037, D1039, D1042, D1049, D1050, D1052, D1059, D3031, D3032, D3598, D3954, D3962, D4003, D4004, D7008, D7015, D7022, D7023   Total: 66.

Old Oak usually had a handful of freight locomotives on its allocation but these were not often stabled inside the shed; they and visiting freight types were commonly seen on the lines around the coaling stage, as here on Sunday 18th September 1960. Four BR Standard Cl. 9F 2-10-0s and one Stanier Cl.8F 2-8-0 are stabled and sandwiching a pannier tank. No.92214 was built at Swindon in October 1959 and after a few weeks at Cardiff Canton, transferred to Banbury shed, its home when the picture was captured on film. In November 1961 the 9F was reallocated to Newport, Ebbw Junction from where, in May/ June 1964, it was loaned to Bath Green Park shed to help with traffic over the Somerset & Dorset main line and may indeed have been the last 9F to operate over that route. Following that, No.92214 was transferred to Severn Tunnel Junction, from where it was withdrawn in August 1965 after the disgustingly short life of less than six years. Saved for preservation, the 9F today works on the Great Central Railway at Loughborough. The Stanier 8F was also built at Swindon, emerging in September 1943 for allocation to St. Philips Marsh. By the beginning of BR the engine was at Cricklewood transferring in August 1955 back to St. Philips Marsh. In January 1960 it was allocated to 81A and relocated in October 1962 to Stourbridge Junction then to Springs Branch in July 1966. A final transfer in December 1967 took No.48410 to Rose Grove where it was withdrawn on the last day of BR steam – 4th August 1968! *N.W. Skinner (ARPT)*

On standby duty beside the 1950-built office block at Old Oak, are 'Castle' No.5066 SIR FELIX POLE and 'Hall' No.6961 STEDHAM HALL. No.5066 came out of Swindon in July 1937 with the name WARDOUR CASTLE and spent all of its working life based at 81A, and although the picture was taken on Thursday 16th August 1962, the 4-6-0 was withdrawn during the next month. No.5066 was renamed in April 1956 and was fitted with a double chimney exactly three years later. Wardour Castle dates from 1390 and is situated in a rural area some fifteen miles west of Salisbury, Wiltshire. It was unique in Britain for its hexagonal planform and was damaged during the English Civil War. The substantial remains survived though and are today in the care of English Heritage. Sir Felix Pole (1st February 1877 – 15th January 1956), is commemorated as the Chairman of the Great Western Railway 1920–1929, having risen from a 14-years old telegraph lad at Swindon. No.6961 was built at Swindon in March 1944 and ran un-named until July 1948. Transferred to Old Oak from Reading in May 1952, STEDHAM HALL never again left the London Division, with later allocations to Southall, Didcot and Oxford, before being withdrawn in September 1965. Stedham Hall itself is near Midhurst, Sussex and dates from 1520, being extended over the years. It was completely renovated from 1910 and is today, converted into high-quality apartments. *David J. Dippie.*

Also gracing Old Oak's rails on 16th August 1961 was 'Hall' No.6923 CROXTETH HALL standing among the ever-present piles of ash among the sidings around Old Oak's coaling stage. No.6923 was quite similar to No.6961, discussed in the previous caption, in that after building in July 1941, the locomotive ran, un-named until August 1946. Also it never strayed from the London Division, going first to Didcot, moving to Reading in November 1950 and in the picture, carries the appropriate 81D shed plate. A final move came in March 1963, to Oxford, with withdrawal from there in December 1965. Croxteth Hall, near Liverpool was the ancestral home of the Molyneux family, the Earls of Sefton. It dates from 1575, being later expanded several times, before it came into the care of Liverpool City Council in 1972. The council sold some of the grounds then opened the remainder of the parkland, and the house, to the public. *David J. Dippie.*

Another type of locomotive long associated with Old Oak Common, was the 61xx 2-6-2 tank engine. Developed specifically for London area suburban services the 6100s were a logical extension of the Class 5101 'Large Prairie' but with a 225psi boiler, which gave the locomotives a tractive effort of 27,340 lbs, about the same as a Hall 4-6-0! Built in batches between April 1931 and November 1935, all seventy of the type went to London Division sheds, and all were still within that Division on the last day of the GWR. During the BR era some of the engines were drafted away, more or less to all areas, but the vast majority remained stationed in and around the Capital until the end. Here is No.6157 at its home shed of Old Oak on Tuesday 23rd August 1960, its clean condition and slight decoration of the edges of the smokebox number plate being an indication of the *esprit de corps* of the crews in 81A's suburban passenger links. The locomotives were inevitably smartly turned out and it is your scribe's experience that they were also very smartly driven – their blazing exhaust sound as they rattled their 6-coach suburban trains past the famous footbridge at Old Oak Common is with me still! No.6157 came out of Swindon in March 1933 and went first to Old Oak. In BR times the engine went from Slough, via Reading and Didcot, to return to 81A in November 1959. By then most of the suburban services had been dieselised so in July 1961 the six-coupled tank made its last move, to Taunton, from where it was withdrawn in May 1962. Happily, No.6106 of the type has been preserved and may be seen at the Great Western Society's Didcot museum. *David J. Dippie.*

With only five months to go before being withdrawn, Didcot shed's 'County' No.1015 COUNTY OF GLOUCESTER joins a 'Modified Hall' and a double-chimney 'Castle' on Old Oak's coal road on Sunday 3rd June 1962. Built at Swindon in March 1946, No.1015 went first to Old Oak, un-named; it would receive its nameplates thirteen months later. The engine remained at 81A until February 1951 when it transferred to Plymouth Laira shed, where it stayed until reallocation to Swindon in September 1959. COUNTY OF GLOUCESTER's final move, to Didcot, occurred in August 1961. *N.W. Skinner (ARPT).*

The driver of 'Castle' No.4098 KIDWELLY CASTLE keeps a good look-out as he backs his engine into the gloom of Old Oak Common's southeast turntable shed. Built in July 1926 the locomotive's first posting was to Old Oak, but by Nationalisation it was at Newton Abbot, where it remained until June 1962 and reallocation to 81A. Whether the chalked train reporting number E60, seen on Thursday 16th August 1962, referred to a service the 4-6-0 had just hauled, or an earlier foray is not known, but No.4098 carried on until December 1963 when it was withdrawn after thirty-seven years' service. The fortress Kidwelly Castle had its origins in Norman times but the present, remaining ruin dates from between 1200 and the latter 1400s. It was frequently involved in the wars between England and the Welsh, led by <u>Owain Glyndŵr</u>, but was not much troubled during the English Civil War, when so many other castles were totally or partially destroyed. The substantial remains, dramatically perched on the bank of the River Gwendraeth, are today managed by Cadw – Welsh Heritage. *David J. Dippie.*

As far as is known, 4300 Class No.6379 spent its working life in the London Division, going first to Old Oak in July 1921. At the end of the GWR it was at Reading, moving to Oxford in April 1954, returning to Reading ten months later. From there it went to Didcot in September 1957, its home depot when this picture was taken. Transferring again to Reading in June 1961, the 2-6-0 was reallocated to Didcot exactly two years later, to be withdrawn during the following August 1963. Behind the locomotive can be seen a concrete post and slat fence which ran along the towpath of the Grand Union Canal. For those without visit permits, the canal towpath was the way into Old Oak – look at the missing slats at left. One wonders who caused that! *David J. Dippie.*

Then based at Plymouth Laira, 4700 class No.4705 rests with a BR 9F and a 'Castle', by the coaling stage. Built in April 1922, by 1948 the 2-8-0 was 'on the books' at Old Oak, which it left in January 1957 for Laira. No.4705 moved away from Devon, to Southall, in September 1962, in a final reallocation it came back to Old Oak in September 1963. Three months later the 2-8-0 was withdrawn. *David J. Dippie.*

As remarked earlier, Old Oak Common was a true 'cathedral of steam' with the interior providing wonderful vistas. Here we present three iconic former Great Western locomotives at rest inside the quadruple turntable building. *(above)* Probably the most famous GWR locomotive ever, No.3440 CITY OF TRURO, on Saturday 17th May 1958, prior to hauling the *DAFFODIL EXPRESS* rail tour the following day, sharing the duty with Caprotti Standard Cl.5 No.73132. Famous of course for the nowadays disputed 100+mph run on 9th May 1904, the locomotive was also significant in that it was the 2000th engine built at Swindon, in May 1903, with its first number 3440. Renumbered 3717 in December 1912, the 4-4-0 was withdrawn in March 1931 to be preserved, after which its history is too well recorded to repeat here. The second image *(opposite, top)* features 'King' No.6000 KING GEORGE V sporting the bell presented when in August 1927 it attended the centenary of the Baltimore & Ohio Railroad in the USA. Emerging from Swindon Works in June 1927, by 1948 it was based at Plymouth Laira depot, transferring from there, via Bristol, Bath Road (December 1948), to Old Oak in September 1952. Fitted with a double chimney in December 1956, No.6000 remained at Old Oak until withdrawal on 3rd December 1962, having covered 1.91 million miles in service. Subsequently preserved, this is another locomotive that does not need its recent history to be repeated here. King George V (3rd June 1865 – 20th January 1936) reigned from the death of his father, Edward VII on 6th May 1910, to his own death. Finally *(opposite, bottom)* we have the Great Western's 'Royal' engine, 'Castle' No.4082 WINDSOR CASTLE, recorded on film on Sunday 7th October 1962 – except that is not exactly true! Built in April 1924, No.4082 was undergoing overhaul in Swindon Works, when in February 1952, it was required to haul the funeral train of the just deceased King George VI. So it exchanged name and number with 7013 BRISTOL CASTLE, and that change never was reversed. So the engine seen here was built in July 1948 and it would remain in as-built condition until withdrawal from Gloucester Horton Road shed, in February 1965, sixteen years and six months old. The previous WINDSOR CASTLE, as 7013 BRISTOL CASTLE, would be fitted with a 4-row superheater and double chimney in May 1958 and she too would be withdrawn from Gloucester, in September 1964, at the age of forty years and five months. Nothing needs to be said about the building, Windsor Castle, used as a royal residence today, but Bristol Castle deserves some mention. Dating from William the Conqueror's time and strategically sited above the River Avon, the castle was much involved in wars, murder, imprisonment and intrigue, but by the mid-1500s was in decline. The remains were demolished in 1656 on the orders of Oliver Cromwell and today, the scant remnants are partially grassed-over in an area of Bristol area known as Castle Park. *Images on this page and opposite bottom C. J. B. Sanderson (ARPT), opposite top David J. Dippie.*

WILLESDEN

To deal with London's burgeoning goods traffic, the London & North Western Railway (LNWR), provided a twelve road, dead ended shed at Willesden Junction in 1873. Covered by three of Mr Ramsbottom's standard hipped roofs, the shed serviced the many locomotives working into, and out of, the expanding goods yards and carriage sheds between Willesden and Stonebridge Park. The first extension came in 1898 when the depot was lengthened at its front end, the new section, however, being covered by a Webb design, northlight roof. The LNWR carried out late improvement works in 1920/1, mainly centred round a mechanical coaling plant and ash towers, before the second and final extension of accommodation occurred in October 1929. That was when the LNWR's successor, the LMS, opened a square plan-form turntable shed adjacent to the rear, northeast corner of the twelve-road building. At about the same time, the first shed's 1898 northlight roof was removed as it had become a maintenance liability, but parts of its associated side walls were retained.

There, pretty much, matters rested. The LMS gave the depot code number 2 then from 1935, it was designated 1A. That was retained through BR times until the shed closed on 27th September 1965, with the 92-years old, hipped roofs still *in situ* though with later cladding and smoke vents. The site was quickly cleared and utilised for Willesden Freightliner Terminal, a purpose that continues today.

Looking south towards the roundhouse on 29th September 1957. Coaling plant on the left, straight shed extreme right. Enthusiasts stepping to one side to allow a Class 5 out of the stabling sidings! Yes, it was another Sunday. *N.W. Skinner (ARPT).*

Willesden – What was on shed Wednesday 16th April 1952:

40006, 40009, 40018, 40019, 40044, 40050, 40052, 40055, 40135, 40204, 41305, 41306, 41909, 42783, 42787, 42812, 42870, 42931, 42940, 42950, 44208, 44442, 44451, 44497, 44683, 44684, 44844, 44870, 44875, 45025, 45035, 45064, 45072, 45089, 45097, 45218, 45327, 45344, 45431, 45437, 45511, 45591, 45593, 45625, 45638, 45676, 45736, 45740, 46142, 46151, 47302, 47412, 47474, 47491, 47531, 47675, 48112, 48122, 48147, 48166, 48171, 48195, 48219, 48368, 48370, 48416, 48433, 48440, 48445, 48476, 48526, 48628, 48658, 48659, 48694, 48722, 49122, 49164, 49180, 49277, 49304, 49344, 58177, 90662, 10001   Total: 85

Oh what a sight; two Stanier Pacifics posing together after topping off their tenders at the coaler on Tuesday 6th June 1961. No.46240 CITY OF COVENTRY (Camden) appears to be in a reasonable external condition whereas sister No.46228 DUCHESS OF RUTLAND (Crewe North) is quite the opposite. The roundhouse is in the right background with the power station at Stonebridge Park on the left. *Norman Preedy*.

'COVENTRY' again, but this time looking even more dapper on the 8th March 1964 on the shed yard. However, nobody has fixed a 1A shed plate and probably never would even though the 8P was now part of Willesden's stud. The transfer from Camden took place during the previous September and from the 29th of that month to 1st December the Pacific was placed in store. Thereafter the usefulness of No.46240 was brought to the fore and she remained in traffic to the end which came on 12th September 1964 at the end of the summer timetable. *Norman Preedy*.

The Willesden shed yard on the evening of Saturday 20th June 1964, with a mainly Stanier feel amongst the locomotives on view. Even the BR Std. 5 had Stanier influences because it was based on the Black 5! Miraculously the original hipped pitched roofs of the shed survived to the end. *Norman Preedy.*

Not satisfied with being the dirtiest engine visiting Willesden shed, 'Britannia' No.70012 JOHN OF GAUNT tries to make the surrounding area just as filthy. Although the Pacific transferred to Willesden from the Eastern Region in April 1963, it relocated to Crewe North during the first month of 1965. However, this image is dated 20th June 1964 but No.70012 is wearing a 5A shed plate, the cast iron kind besides the coating of ...? *Norman Preedy.*

Willesden – What was on shed Sunday 27th January 1957:
40007, 40016, 40019, 40042, 40044, 40046, 40047, 40051, 40053, 40064, 40066, 40461, 41320, 42118, 42487, 42783, 42812, 42814, 42852, 42870, 42885, 42923, 43024, 44067, 44116, 44372, 44680, 44763, 44771, 44838, 44869, 44873, 44893, 44916, 44941, 44949, 45019, 45021, 45024, 45027, 45032, 45035, 45051, 45089, 45128, 45139, 45185, 45255, 45350, 45374, 45434, 45445, 45510, 45513, 45517, 45547, 45669, 45735, 45740, 45742, 46168, 46431, 47342, 47349, 47474, 47475, 47492, 47499, 47505, 47515, 47520, 47675, 48020, 48074, 48129, 48171, 48249, 48305, 48332, 48416, 48476, 48518, 48603, 48656, 48705, 48716, 49078, 49088, 49122, 49270, 49321, 12033, 12034, 12036, 12049, 12078, 13018, 13019, 13050, DELTIC   Total: 100.

Another 'Brit' simply because it was there! They had to feature big in these albums because they were not partisan; No.70034 THOMAS HARDY one of those made redundant on the ER and transferred to Willesden in April 1963. Now this one had been everywhere except the WR by the time it reached 1A and now it was about to venture north by relocating to Crewe North where amongst other things its reasonable external appearance would change, for the worse! Its ultimate destination was a scrapyard in Scotland where it ended up after withdrawal on 6th May 1967. Before then it had a few more sheds to reside in – Crewe South, Newton Heath, and Carlisle Kingmoor. *Norman Preedy*.

A nice scene recorded on Sunday afternoon, 26th March 1961 beneath the thirty-year old coaling plant with 'Jubilee' No.45672 ANSON of apparent no fixed abode, and resident 3F No.47501. The 6P was a recent arrival from Kingmoor and has yet to acquire a shed plate. *C.J.B. Sanderson (ARPT)*.

Thursday 27ᵗʰ May 1954 – A visit to the IRS Willesden Exhibition found:
10203, 13046, 10100, 11700, 11109, 18000, 92014, 71000, 80084, 70037, 73050, 77009, 84019, 27002.

The running sheds and yards contained the following:
12004, 12032, 40001, 40002, 40049, 40066, 42155, 42787, 42948, 42966, 44372, 44680, 44768, 44873, 45003, 45024, 45027, 45148, 45149, 45187, 45237, 45301, 45321, 45374, 45398, 45495, 45544, 45591, 46126, 46165, 46254, 47491, 48122, 48129, 48295, 48474, 48476, 49180, 49275, 75031, 75037, 80034.   *Total 42, not including exhibits.*

(opposite) Three related but undated views of the International Railway Congress exhibition staged by British Railways in the roundhouse at Willesden motive power depot. The exhibits represented the most modern of motive power working on BR. They were stabled in the stalls ranged around the turntable and as can be seen, the turntable had been removed and a false raised floor inserted into the pit. The exhibition ran from Tuesday 25th May to Friday 4th June 1954. What the actual attendance was is unknown. *All images by Ken Cockerill (ARPT).*

We not only have three images from the Willesden exhibition of 1954 but we also have the cast list and a list of those playing secondary roles in the main shed and yard. Not only that, we have these two illustrations of Deltic in the very roundhouse where the exhibition was actually staged. The date of this latter event was 27th January 1957, a Sunday and obviously a time when the big blue diesel was showing its charms off to the LMR. The glow in the background had nothing to do with any angelic presence; it was just daylight trying to penetrate the murk of the building. Ranged around the pit with the Co-Co were a Stanier 5, a 'Patriot', and a 'Jubilee'. The EE lads are taking their jobs seriously as they check their steed inside and out! We are not sure of the actual complexities involved when Deltic was working service trains for the LM or indeed the ER but if our assumptions are correct BR was saving a lot of money in fuel alone by allowing English Electric to show off the prowess of the diesel in order to get orders for the 3,300 h.p. machine. Finally, in contrast to the 1954 images, look at the turntable pit and floor of the shed – quite a difference wouldn't you say? *Chris Dunne.*

Ivatt Cl.2 No.46509 pokes out of the straight shed on 22nd May 1965. This class was associated with 1A since their introduction and in 1965 the final four of a long line of them – 46507, 46508, 46509, and 46512 – were still finding work but their days were really numbered. *Ken Groundwater (ARPT). (below)* Here is Stanier 'Crab' No.42958 on Willesden shed 28th October 1962 when full lining was still being applied to these engines and their tenders. The Nuneaton shed plate tells us that the date is correct because in June 1962 it was ex-Birkenhead. Although a number of these engines had been allocated to Willesden in the early days of the class and indeed during early BR days, latterly they were all at other former Western Division depots. This particular 2-6-0 had never been allocated to 1A its only London shed phase was at Kentish Town when new from January to October 1934. *K.H. Cockerill (ARPT).*

Willesden – What was on shed Sunday 24th May 1959:
40010, 40043, 40044, 40060, 40064, 40066, 40068, 42118, 42350, 42351, 42359, 42360, 42365, 42366, 42368, 42422, 42430, 42463, 42482, 42576, 42604, 42627, 42747, 42812, 42859, 42870, 42885, 42889, 42947, 44058, 44208, 44497, 44746, 44825, 44834, 44838, 44845, 44870, 44875, 44906, 44943, 45050, 45111, 45252, 45278, 45288, 45301, 45350, 45375, 45387, 45427, 45500, 45510, 45511, 45554, 45592, 45603, 45613, 45625, 45655, 45734, 45740, 46147, 46246, 46458, 47315, 47482, 47483, 47486, 47501, 48122, 48128, 48201, 48256, 48258, 48318, 48335, 48375, 48416, 48435, 48440, 48476, 48545, 48551, 48600, 48601, 48624, 48632, 48649, 48665, 48668, 48722, 49070, 49122, 49164, 49277, 49344, 90696, 92018, 10000, 10001, 10201, D210, 12073, 12100, 13015, D3016, D3050, D3177, D8017, D8201, D8202, D8208   Total: 113.

Ivatt Cl.4 No.43063 was, as can be clearly seen, allocated to Heaton Mersey, a shed which rarely, if ever, had a duty which would bring one of its charges down the WCML to London. One of the BR Doncaster built members of the class, No.43063 started life at New England shed in November 1950, it then moved across country to Woodford in June 1956 for what turned out to be another six-year stint before transferring to Saltley in March 1962. Continuing to make a lazy circle towards its place of building, the 2-6-0 upped-sticks after six months in Birmingham and went to Heaton Mersey on the old Cheshire Lines system. It was from there that the Cl.4 found its way to Willesden on Saturday 22nd May 1965. Now, is that a Southern Region marker hanging on the smokebox? The plot thickens! The how and why to its journey some 200 miles from its home shed is probably lost in time but if somebody knows different then please drop a line to the publisher quoting this title – we would like to hear from you. Oh yes, the Ivatt moved on yet again north and eastwards but didn't quite make it to Doncaster and ended up working its days out from North Blyth shed August 1966 to September 1967. Note the tablet catcher cut-out in the tender side sheet for working on the M&GNJR. *Ken Groundwater (ARPT)*.

Parallel boiler 'Scots' were becoming hard to find by 1953 but this little beauty was recorded at Willesden that year. No.46156 THE SOUTH WALES BORDERER was finally rebuilt and fitted with a taper boiler during the spring of 1954. The engine had acquired a Stanier tender as long ago as 1936. *S.C.Crook (ARPT)*.

SR Pacifics worked into Willesden on many occasions (*see* later) but six-coupled dock tanks from Southampton were quite rare visitors and I hasten to add that probably none of them had ever been to 1A before. That changed on 4th September 1955 when USA 3F 0-6-0T No.30066 paid a visit whilst en route elsewhere. Here it is near the roundhouse looking rather grotty but unmistakably wearing the 71I shed plate denoting Southampton Docks shed. The lower illustration shows that the thirteen year old tank, which wasn't in steam, had been tucked away on a siding at the base of the water tank next to the roundhouse. The *Railway Observer* reported that two of the USA tanks had been sent on loan to the LMR. One of them, No.30061 was initially seen at Acton (N&SWJ) on 1st September en route to Kentish Town where it's only reported activity was a spell of shunting at Somers Town. Meanwhile, No.30066 stayed overnight at Bletchley (its presence at 1A wasn't reported in the *RO*) on 8th September and was noted passing Rugby next day. It had got to Bank Hall shed early the following week. No.30066 was reported as being quite well received at 27A but was en route back to the SR on 28th October when spotted at Rugby, job done! *Clive Allen & Clive Allen son & father.*

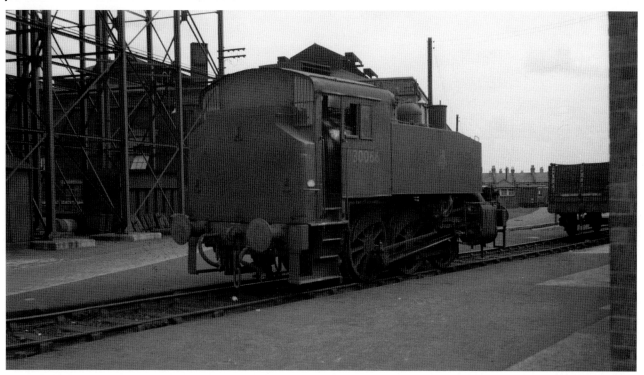

An un-named and totally unkempt 'Patriot' on the shed yard on 24th August 1957. This is No.45517, one of Willesden's own at least it was from June 1953 to July 1958 when it transferred to Bank Hall to work the Liverpool (Central) to Newcastle expresses, and appearing decidedly cleaner than this. *David J. Dippie.*

What a difference a year (or near as damn it) makes! No.45517 on 3rd May 1958 looking rather plush now just prior to its transfer up north! *W.R.E. Lewis (ARPT).*

Willesden – What was on shed Saturday 24th February 1962:

40006, 40010, 40042, 40049, 40080, 40144, 40157, 40201, 42071, 42117, 42350, 42368, 42470, 42478, 42576, 42585, 42604, 42627, 42747, 42785, 42810, 42870, 42976, 44348, 44364, 44710, 44780, 45027, 45078, 45114, 45184, 45191, 45196, 45276, 45278, 45297, 45374, 45552, 45583, 45735, 46146, 46161, 46205, 46207, 46424, 47304, 47355, 47501, 48147, 48171, 48204, 48350, 48366, 48384, 48518, 48531, 48544, 48551, 48601, 48610, 48624, 48628, 48629, 48632, 48649, 48668, 49413, 49431, 70004, 70017, 70021, 70033, 70047, 75030, 75052, 10000, 10001, 10201, 10202, 10203, D3016, D3173, D5021, D5024, D5031, D5077, D5078, D8002, D8004, D8035, D8040   Total: 91.

As already mentioned, SR Pacifics were no strangers to Willesden, the trick as far as caption writers are concerned is finding out the reasons why they were visiting in the first instance. Rebuilt 'West Country' No.34100 APPLEDORE from Salisbury was photographed on a damp 14th November 1964 on a working totally unrelated to football, rugby, hockey, or indeed any sport – probably! A shed plate was more than likely never fitted. The top image shows the Pacific with the straight shed and cooling towers as a backdrop whilst the lower one reveals the rear end with the roundhouse and water towers as the background. Let's use a visitor to show us around the depot. *both Mike Shannon*.

Un-rebuilt WC No.34045 OTTERY ST.MARY takes on water on 24th August 1957. Found any connections yet? *David J. Dippie*.

With some fancy material secured around the chimneys a pair of ex-LMS tanks wait for their fate at Willesden on 28th October 1962. *Howard Foster*.

Resident Stanier 8F No.48171 on one of the coaling roads 7ᵗʰ October 1962! *C.J.B. Sanderson (ARPT).*

Another resident 8F on the same day, No.48600 coupled to one of those parallel high-sided tenders which were neither one thing nor another. This tender No.4573, a 3500 gallons type with seven tons coal capacity, was coupled to the 8F from November 1958; it had been built for 'Jubilee' No.5616. *C.J.B. Sanderson (ARPT).*

Out in the wilderness! Three out of favour ex-LMS tank engines dumped on the perimeters of Willesden m.p.d. Sunday 7th October 1962: top to bottom – Nos.42221, 40201, 42470. *All C.J.B. Sanderson (ARPT).*

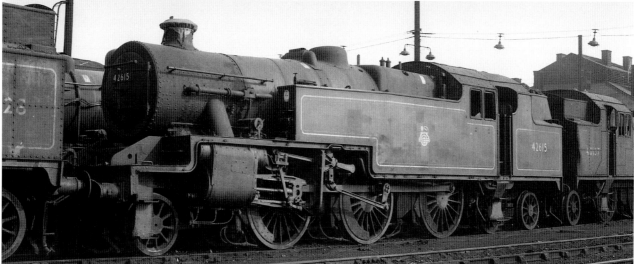

In amongst it – same day! *All C.J.B. Sanderson (ARPT)*.

Bring on the Scots! No.46146 THE RIFLE BRIGADE enjoys the weekend sojourn on 7th October 1962. Another resident, No.46111 ROYAL FUSILIER rests in semi-shade but is just as prepared on that same Sunday in October 1962. *Both C.J.B. Sanderson. (ARPT).*

Yes, Carnforth shed was short of cleaners – how did you know? An afternoon arrival on the shed yard, en route to the roundhouse after being given a pile of clack at the coaler! 'Jubilee' No.45606, with one of those fabulous empirical names known and remembered by every railway enthusiast throughout the land – except the GWR/WR chaps who didn't know that other locomotives plied this wonderful country – as one of those far off bits of empire. In 1982 it was only former railway enthusiasts and about 1% of the population who knew where that certain group of islands known as the FALKLAND ISLANDS were actually situated. *C.J.B. Sanderson (ARPT)*.

Between the sheds! 'Patriot' No.45524 BLACKPOOL is turned, coaled and watered on 6th June 1959. The finish isn't bad either. This was one of Camden's fleet which had been along to the main shed for some reason. Note the chalked triangle on the buffer beam; was that signifying something? *C.J.B. Sanderson (ARPT)*.

Willesden – What was on shed Sunday 28th April 1963:

41239, 42068, 42071, 42077, 42100, 42103, 42106, 42118, 42218, 42221, 42234, 42336, 42350, 42431, 42478, 42573, 42577, 42611, 42616, 42707, 42960, 43018, 44840, 44844, 45020, 45044, 45116, 45198, 45288, 45305, 45530, 45586, 45620, 45655, 45666, 45735, 46123, 46221, 46229, 46246, 46255, 46423, 46472, 46504, 46505, 46506, 46517, 47307, 47501, 48134, 48247, 48252, 48345, 48356, 48445, 48506, 48551, 48628, 48649, 48657, 70000, 70004, 70010, 70018, 70024, 70031, 70032, 70034, 70043, 70048, 73004, 73014, 73033, 90084, 90104, 92075, 10001, 12101, D3018, D3173, D3795, D3796, D3797, D5000, D5013, D5016, D5021, D5023, D5024, D5028, D5029, D5030, D5031, D5035, D5075, D5077, D5078, D5081, D5135, D5138, D5144, D5145, D8005, D8006, D8009, D8035, D8036   Total: 107.

Of course, it wouldn't be Willesden without this gang of diesel-electrics: The date is 16th June 1959 and the LMS pair Nos.10000 and 10001 *(above)* were coupled together with the connecting doors open and those gangways in which so much faith and design was entrusted for the early diesel fleet, was stretched across the gap. As things worked out those diesels built with these connections had them removed, and the doors welded up, within a couple of years in traffic. Such was the draught nuisance, coupled with the fact that most diesel locomotives could handle the traffic loads without double-heading (a nice idea but no thanks!). Next in line *(below)* 10201 which was a typical Southern design right down to the shrill warning whistle; the bogie design was later used by English Electric for the 200 Type 4s they built for BR whilst BR themselves modelled their Type 4 bogies on these for the Sulzer diesels. All the diesels were rated 5P. *Both C.J.B. Sanderson (ARPT).*

NEASDEN

In 1897, in anticipation of the opening of its extension to London, the Manchester, Sheffield and Lincolnshire Railway (MSLR), adopted the more appropriate title of Great Central Railway (GCR). The GCR line into London finally came into use on 25th July 1898 for goods traffic and 15th March 1899 for passenger, but because the Marylebone terminus was somewhat cramped the GCR's locomotive shed had to be sited some miles out, at Neasden. This was a six road dead-end building in brick, with a northlight roof of twenty transverse ridges. Along the eastern side were ranged the depot offices, a repair shop with wheel drop and other ancillary spaces; in the rear yard at the east side, a 'Goliath' sheerlegs was installed while the shed's front yard was equipped with a turntable and ramped coaling stage and, for many years, a huge coal stack.

The LNER succeeded the GCR and carried out some improvements at Neasden shed, including provision of a mechanical coaling tower in the 1930s. However, because the depot originally had been laid out on former smallholdings and allotments, largely occupying soft ground, the new coaling plant eventually suffered from foundation problems so at the beginning of the 1950s it was replaced with another, larger structure, more firmly placed on deep pilings, after which, the first mechanical coaler was removed. All through this the original, ramped coaling stage remained as a support for the depot's water tank, but it could be – and was – utilised as a standby fuelling source when the mechanical device was out of use for some reason.

Coded NEA by the LNER, the depot was re-designated 34E by British Railways, Eastern Region, before being transferred to the London Midland Region in February 1958, with a new code of 14D, following which the LNER influence was removed as quickly and thoroughly as possible. Whoever was in charge though, locomotives based at Neasden covered the fairly sparse express passenger, though buoyant freight, services over the main line, but Marylebone's suburban passenger workings into the Chilterns were quite intense and thus became an early candidate for dieselisation. In a wider sense British Railways determined that the former GCR Extension line to London was surplus to requirements so in 1966 it was closed north of Aylesbury basically, after a few years of a most depressing run-down. Neasden shed had succumbed earlier, on 18th June 1962, after which the site became a coal concentration depot for a time. Today, the site of the engine shed and yard is covered by housing and a large aggregate plant.

When the GCR built its line into London it erected carriage and wagon works at Neasden, the former of six roads and also part-employed as a carriage shed. The wagon shop was smaller and adjacent to the carriage building both being situated on the other (north) side of what became the North Circular Road, from the engine shed. With all the wood that necessarily would be stored in such places it can be no surprise that the LNER tried out Sentinel steam locomotives as pilots – the first occasion being 1924/5 when two Y6 were tested, but not continued with. The carriage shed lost its roof due to war damage; it was not replaced and

indeed, the remaining side walls were demolished leaving open roads and ancillary buildings; the wagon shop was unscathed. Sentinels returned in 1941 with four different machines being employed in the years up to the end of 1947, from when a single Y3, No.8172, remained until being withdrawn in December 1951, after lying out of use for some months; it never received the 6 prefix for its allotted BR number. The Sentinel's replacement was an ex-GNR 0-6-0T of LNER Class J50, No.68949 which arrived in May 1951, but was not really successful (disliked by the men most probably!) so it left again in January 1952. Later shunting at the carriage and wagon complexes was usually a Class N5 0-6-2T job until the coming of 0-6-0 diesel locomotives, of which Neasden received new Darlington-built diesel-electric Nos.13304, 13305, and 13306 in early May 1956 followed on 13th October by diesel-mechanical types Nos.11114 and 11155 from Kings Cross. The DM types transferred away to Crewe South on 6th September 1958 whilst the larger DE trio were called to Cricklewood over a year later on 14th November 1959. Here we see Neasden's last Sentinel, No.8172 (Works No.8323 of September 1930), among some ancient tool vans and seemingly laid up, on Friday 28th May 1948. Your scribe although very young, does recall seeing the 0-4-0T at work in what must have been 1949/50, but eventually it went to Doncaster where it was condemned, as noted above, in December 1951. *K.H. Cockerill (ARPT)*.

Neasden – What was on shed Saturday 26th April 1952:

43127, 60049, 60051, 60061, 60107, 60111, 60863, 60966, 61028, 61083, 61163, 61164, 64438, 67416, 67753, 67762, 67769, 67772, 67781, 67782, 67785, 67786, 67796, 69060, 69065, 69302, 69315, 69341, 69519, 69541, 69560, 69814, 69828   Total: 33.

These two pictures are contrasting views of locomotive number 67418. At top, still in LNER livery and looking quite spruce, C13 (GCR Class 9K) No.7418, basks in the sunlit yard of Neasden shed on Friday 28th May 1948; note the long-handled shovel and fire iron stored on their special brackets above the side tank. First introduced in 1903 the type was Mr Robinson's first suburban tank design for the GCR. Initially most went to Neasden shed but were gradually moved away when Class A5 (GCR 9N) 4-6-2T began to appear from 1911. However, two or three C13s were kept at Neasden for working the Chalfont – Chesham branch for which they were subsequently fitted with push-pull apparatus – fittings for that vacuum operated system are seen on the side of 7418's smokebox. In the lower picture, taken Sunday 7th October 1956, the engine was in its BR livery as No.67418, but looking out of use and a bit tired, as it shared a siding with a WD 2-8-0. Built at Gorton Works in September 1903, No.67418 was a Neasden-based locomotive for all of its BR time, together with sister No.67420 and from March 1951 No.67416. Usually one engine was at Neasden undergoing routine maintenance while the other one, or two, were out-stationed at Rickmansworth sub-shed, a situation pertaining up to withdrawal of all three in December 1958. Their replacements for the Chesham branch were three auto-fitted, LMS Ivatt Class 2 six-coupled tanks. Of points to note, in the top image, Neasden's breakdown train can be seen on its customary siding on the west side of the shed yard; here also were parked stored locomotives and from time to time the rails were flanked by a large coal stack. The bottom image gives a good view of Neasden's original ramped coaling stage with the water tank atop, which held around 65000 gallons; the shed's turntable on its own spur, is out of picture, to the left. *(top) K.H. Cockerill (ARPT)* and *(below) C.J.B. Sanderson (ARPT)*.

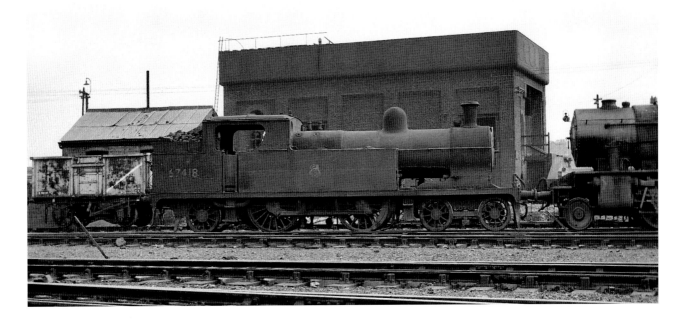

A most interesting locomotive is seen near the sheerlegs at Neasden shed on Friday 28th May 1948, just five months before it was withdrawn, without receiving its BR number of 69077. LNER Class M2 No.9077 had been built in February 1916 by the Yorkshire Engine Company, as Metropolitan Railway Class G, No.96. Unusual for a tank engine in being named – this 0-6-4T for its designer, Charles Jones – the type was intended for mixed traffic work, but in reality they spent most of their time in goods haulage. All Metropolitan Railway steam locomotives not taken over by the London Passenger Transport Board (LPTB) were transferred to the LNER on 1st November 1937 though most did not stray from their home at Neasden, being simply moved to the LNER shed. When ex-Met locomotives required heavy repair they were sent to the ex-GER, Stratford Works – in fact that is where this engine would be scrapped. Here it would seem that No.9077 had a problem with the front driving axle requiring a light repair, but given its short future, it is quite likely the engine did not again turn a wheel in service. At right is the back door of the shed, through which visitors without permits could usually gain unimpeded access; your scribe wishes he had a Pound for every time he slipped in that way, over the years! At left are seen the cooling towers of the coal-fired, Taylors Lane, Power Station, 1903 – 1972. *K.H. Cockerill (ARPT).*

This picture of L3 (GCR Class 1B/ LNER Class L1 [to 1945]) 2-6-4T, No.69060 is particularly valuable as it provides a rare glimpse of Neasden's second mechanical coaling plant being built – the unstable predecessor lies just beyond. The photograph dates from early in 1950 and shows a typically grubby (!) Neasden engine in early BR livery with front buffer beam number, though its 34E shed plate, having been in place, is missing. Mr Robinson's Class B1 was the first design of 2-6-4T in Britain and because of their ungainly appearance they were nicknamed 'Crabs!' No.69060 left Gorton Works in June 1916 as

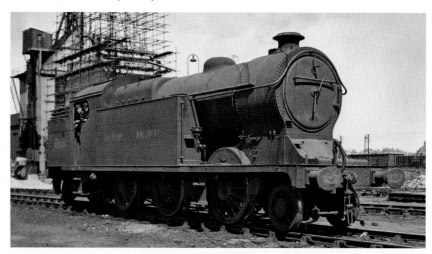

No.341 and headed for Neasden from where it worked until being transferred to Woodford in late March 1929. Thereafter it returned to Neasden no less than three times the first two occasions for a couple of years each but the final residency saw the big tank doing a near twelve-year stint before moving away totally to King's Cross on the last day of May 1953. It transferred to Frodingham just three weeks after moving over to 34A and was withdrawn from 36C a year later. For some reason the engine must have had an affinity with London because it came back and got a job as Stationary Boiler at Stratford works until it was condemned in August 1957. As if to finish the connection, No.69060 was cut up at Stratford. *C.J.B. Sanderson (ARPT)*

For a few Saturdays, March – May every year, up to the beginning of the 60s, Neasden was Britain's most cosmopolitan depot, where engines from all four pre-Nationalisation companies could be seen together. The occasions were the annual matches at Wembley stadium: the Girls' International Hockey, the boys' International football, the rugby league cup final and the football league and FA cup finals – plus other events that brought large crowds to Wembley stadium. Each occasion would see trains from all around the country coming through Neasden with their locomotives laying-over on the shed. Your scribe remembers Schools 4-4-0, B17, B12, Stanier Class 5, Castle and Hall 4-6-0s, Bulled Light Pacifics and once, a very impressive visitor, Peppercorn A1

No.60144 KINGS COURIER. Regrettably, usable pictures of such events have eluded us, but here is an example of those one-off workings that came to Neasden. George Spencer Ltd, of Basford, Nottingham, had arranged a special train exclusively to take employees to visit the Festival of Britain exhibition at London's South Bank. Neither the Thompson B1's number nor the date, were recorded with the photograph, but the Festival ran between 4th May and 30th September 1951, so the picture comes from that period. Just seen is 34E's A5 4-6-2T No.69822, which was built at Gorton in February 1923 and over the years, would spend four stints at Neasden shed: February 1923 – December 1929; November 1937 – May 1938; June 1940 – March 1950 and July 1950 – December 1952. At that final departure it transferred to Colwick and from there in March 1957 to Gorton, where it was withdrawn in November 1958. George Spencer set up his first factory in Basford in 1902, then later others at Hucknall and Lutterworth where his design of knitted material for undergarments became famous, being sold under the name of *Vedonis*. Output was interrupted during WW2 for the production of munitions and George Spencer died in 1946, but production continued to an unknown date. Today the factory buildings still exist in other use and *Vedonis* products are available through a number of on-line outlets, but where they are manufactured is another unknown. *S.C. Crook (ARPT).*

In the very last days of the LNER and through the BR period up to the beginning of 1959, Neasden shed would always be associated with Thompson's Class L1 2-6-4T. Intended to replace such types as Robinson's Class A5 4-6-2T, the first L1 was delivered by Darlington in May 1945, remaining the only example until 1948, when Darlington built twenty-nine more and outside contractors, North British Locomotive Co. (NBL) and Robert Stephenson & Hawthorn (RSH), added another seventy, between 1948 and 1950.

The L1 was very powerful and its 5ft 2in. wheels made it quick off the mark, both desirable attributes for a locomotive designed for start/stop suburban passenger work. However, the engine men did not much like them, being used to the 'Rolls-Royce' comfort of the A5s, whereas the L1 had a serious flaw in that it suffered greatly from early axle-box wear which made the engines rough riders. So much so, that at Neasden at least, they gained the nickname 'concrete mixers!' Even so, nearly forty were based at 34E by 1950 and in all fifty-eight different engines of the type would spend time at the shed. However, by 1951 BR started trying alternative power, first in the shape of LMS Ivatt Cl.4 2-6-0, then LMS 2-6-4T, of Fowler, Stanier and Fairburn designs, as well as BR Standard Cl.4 2-6-4T. When Neasden shed became a London Midland Region depot, the remaining L1s were soon eradicated, as were the Standards, leaving mainly LMS 2-6-4T to see out the days of steam on Marylebone suburban services. In this image from Sunday 4th July 1954, we see L1 No.67792 at Neasden in company with another of its type and a pair of ex-GCR N5 0-6-2T. The L1 was one of the RSH batch built in June 1950, going first to Hitchin on 28th June then four weeks later to King Cross. For some reason it returned to Darlington but to 51A for a month in April 1951 then went back to 34A. Its introduction to Neasden took place on the last day of August 1952. The 2-6-4T went back to 34A in November 1954, only to return to Neasden in May 1955. On 21st August 1958 No.67792 went yet again to Kings Cross but initially on loan and permanently from 30th November. Three years later on 19th November 1961, the L1 left London for Colwick, from where it was withdrawn on 29th December 1962, just 12 years old. The Neasden L1s travelled a long way for major and intermediate overhauls making the trip to Darlington each time. Non-classified repairs and damage repairs were undertaken at Stratford. *F.W. Hampson (ARPT).*

Also from Sunday 4th July 1954, here is another engine destined to last for only twelve years (*see* previous caption), Ivatt Cl.4 No.43107, was one of a handful of the type tried out on Neasden shed's duties and while the Ivatts did not stay long, their overall design was acceptable and soon after repeated in the BR Standard Class 4 2-6-0 (*see* next caption). No.43107 was built at Doncaster in May 1951 with a first allocation to 31D South Lynn, where it took part in running services over the Midland & Great Northern Joint Railway (M&GNR). It left rural Norfolk in March 1953 for a sixteen-month stint at Neasden before returning to 31D; therefore when this picture was taken the 2-6-0 was about to go back to East Anglia. When the M&GNR closed in March 1959, No.43107 moved to Boston, from where it was taken out of service in December 1963 *F.W. Hampson (ARPT)*

Continuing the theme from the previous two captions about L1 2-6-4T, their prospective replacement types *and* engines having lives of just twelve years; here we see another 4th July 1954 picture, this time of BR Std. Cl.4 No.76035 sandwiched between a WD 2-8-0 and an Ivatt 2-6-0, all backed by Neasden shed's coal stack which randomly came and went over the years. The Standard was not even two months old, having arrived new, from Doncaster Works and by the end of August 1954 she would be joined at 34E by nine sisters, 76036 – 76044. They took their place on Marylebone suburban trains – usually those going furthest out, to Aylesbury and High Wycombe – and they were much appreciated by the men for their comfort, power and speed, so it can be no surprise that all stayed at Neasden shed until it closed in June 1962. Except for this one! In March 1955, No.76035 departed for Hitchin, from where it returned to Neasden sixteen months later. Its next move was when Neasden closed and the 2-6-0 went to nearby Cricklewood, then when *that* depot closed in December 1964, No.76035 went to Willesden, leaving there in May 1965, just before closure of that depot, to go to Chester. There the locomotive's twelve year life came to an end, in December 1966. *F.W. Hampson (ARPT)*

Neasden – What was on shed Saturday 2ⁿᵈ May 1953 (Cup Final Day):
43065, 43066, 43089, 43144, 60063, 60103, 60108, 60111, 61009, 61028, 61077, 61116, 61136, 61151, 61152, 61153, 61156, 61162, 61163, 61174, 61192, 61206, 67416, 67751, 67770, 67773, 67774, 67779, 67792, 67794, 69064, 69060, 69065, 69315, 69318, 69341, 69350, 69814, 90040, 90486, 90638   Total: 41.

An uncommon visitor to Neasden on Wednesday 25th August 1954 was ex-Great Eastern S69 – LNER B12 – No.61570, from Ipswich shed. What brought the 4-6-0 to 34E is not known; a broad search through the internet found nothing for the date, or a day or so each side, either in general, or at Wembley stadium. One possibility and not uncommon in those days, is that the engine hauled a troop train from East Anglia to Neasden, for handing over to a local engine for the onward journey – but that may only be speculated upon. No.61570 was built at Stratford Works in June 1920, as GER 1570 and for all its BR time was an Ipswich engine; it was withdrawn from there in March 1958. The picture gives another good view of Neasden's original coaling plant with its two chutes and some detail of the 1950 mechanical plant. *Christopher Campbell.*

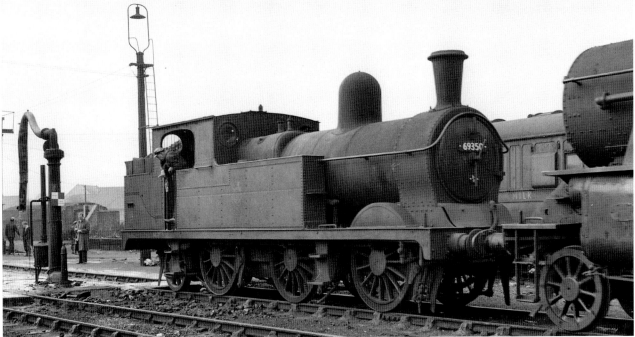

Significant in that it introduced the Belpaire firebox to Britain's railways, Parker's Class N5 (GCR 9C, 9F and 9O) 0-6-2T, would eventually total 131 engines of which 121 came into British Railways' service. Employing them on shunting and trip work, Neasden shed had ten of the type in 1950 but these were gradually whittled down, year by year, until the last three were withdrawn in December 1959, after spending some time in store. In happier times, Sunday 7th October 1956, No.69350 rests in the yard at Neasden while a visiting group of enthusiasts plods about, collecting numbers. This N5 was built by Beyer, Peacock (Works No.4186) in April 1900 and had been allocated to Neasden since October 1946. However, despite being still in use and seemingly not in bad condition, the engine would be withdrawn just three months after the picture was taken. Note in the background how a former milk van had been incorporated into Neasden's breakdown train, still bearing a MILK logo. *C.J.B. Sanderson (ARPT)*

Taking a rest while her two sisters were employed on the Chesham branch trains, auto-fitted C13 No.67416 is stabled in the external repair area, at the southeast corner of Neasden shed; the date is Sunday 3rd March 1957. The illustration features a lot of small detail: the fire irons are missing from their bracket over the side tank – stored for safe keeping, or borrowed for another C13? Just seen is the roughly built wooden shed for keeping tools dry, the springs and their hangers lying on the ground by an oil drum and on the other side of the 4-4-2T, hoses and cables are also dumped at the foot of a lightweight, electrically powered hoist. That triangular hoist would be hinged out from the side of the engine shed, to allow the lifting of heavy items into and out of wagons and through the red painted repair shop doors. No.67416 was built at Gorton in August 1903 and would commence its final posting, to Neasden in March 1951, upon moving from Kings Cross; withdrawal came on 23rd December 1958. A brace of Fairburn 2-6-4T are distantly seen, the nearest being No.42249, which was built at Derby in October 1946 and moved from Plaistow to Neasden in March 1955. The engine was reallocated to Gorton in November 1961, Trafford Park in September 1963, and finally Bolton in November 1964 from where it was withdrawn in July 1966. *C.J.B. Sanderson (ARPT)*

N5 No.69319 lies in store at Neasden in May 1958. The engine is joined by an unidentified sister which must have been either No.69257 or No.69341, as they were the last three of the type to be allocated to 34E since January 1957. No.69319 was built in March 1900 and had earlier been present at Neasden between April 1924 and November 1935, returning in January 1957 from Langwith Junction. The London Midland Region took over the shed in February 1958 so it is a good bet that the N5s were stored soon after that event, if not before. Nevertheless the trio of ex-GCR 0-6-2T managed to survive until all three were withdrawn in December 1959, by which time No.69341 had been a Neasden engine for no less than 40 years and seven months! *A.R. Thompson (ARPT)*

The stored N5 No.69319 is again partly seen in July 1958, joined by 'Jinty' No.47644 and Fairburn 2-6-4T No.42230; in the foreground Neasden's coal stack has been removed and this time it would not be reconstituted. The ex-LMS 0-6-0T came from locomotive builder William Beardmore (392/1929), and was a visitor from Kentish Town depot, having worked over to Neasden from Cricklewood or via the North London line from further east of the Capital. The locomotive had been allocated to Kentish Town for some time, but in February 1960 would move to Derby from where it ended service in November 1962. The Fairburn tank emerged from Derby Works in June 1946 and came to Neasden in April 1955 from Plaistow, remaining until transferred away in December 1961 to Saltley; followed by several stints at sheds in the Midlands before the engine was withdrawn in August 1965, from Manchester's Trafford Park shed. *K. Linford (ARPT)*

The date is Sunday 20th April 1958 and C13 No.67420 has been based at Neasden for nearly seventeen years. It is one of the trio of 4-4-2T retained for working the Chesham branch (see earlier captions) and as was standard practice, this was the one locomotive not in use while her sisters – Nos.67416 and 67418 – were operating from Rickmansworth sub-shed; unusually the C13 is stabled on the siding giving access to the shearlegs. Springs and oil drums continue to litter the area and although it is only two months since the London Midland Region took over Neasden, the new shed code plate has dutifully been affixed to the engine's smokebox door. Built at Gorton in August 1904, No.67420 would be taken out of use eight months after this scene was recorded. See in the distance a BR Class 5 4-6-0 of which Nos.73155 and 73156 were on the shed's roster at the time, but would be moved away in the next month. *F.W. Hampson (ARPT)*

Neasden – What was on shed Sunday 21st July 1957:

42222, 42225, 42230, 42249, 42250, 42251, 42253, 44875, 60877, 60974, 61028, 61116, 61136, 61187, 61866, 65390, 67418, 67420, 67740, 67743, 67748, 67752, 67753, 67758, 67767, 67769, 67795, 69257, 69319, 69341, 73155, 73157, 73159, 76035, 76036, 76037, 76039, 76040, 76043, 76044, 80137, 80138, 80139, 80140, 80141, 80142, 13304, 13305, 13306   Total: 49.

Neasden – What was on shed Sunday 25th February 1962:

42087, 42092, 42250, 42253, 42281, 42291, 44711, 45379, 61116, 61136, 61373, 61897, 61910, 70045, 70048, 73053, 73066, 73156, 73157, 76035, 76036, 76037, 76038, 76040, 76041, 76043, 76044, 76052, 84029, 90065, 12068, D3869   Total: 32.

CRICKLEWOOD

Every main line railway company that served London found in time, that locomotive depots sited near the various termini were insufficient to deal with the huge growth in freight traffic. Accordingly, sites were sought in what were then the outer suburbs, where large goods yards could be laid out, together with attendant engine sheds. Just such a place was Cricklewood, on the Midland Railway (MR) route into London. There, the extensive Brent Up and Down sidings were sited, partly also served by the MR's line to Willesden where it joined the North and Southwest Junction Railway, the 'western circle' so to speak, of London (generically called the West London Extension Railway), and the source of much cross-and-round-London traffic.

The MR erected a square plan-form, gable roof roundhouse at Cricklewood, opening in 1882 followed eleven years later by a second such building, which adjoined the first on its east side, *en echelon*; until 1900 the shed was known as Childs Hill. Freight remained the depot's *raison d'etre* and it served such purpose through MR days coded 15, then into the LMS, when at first it was re-coded 16, under Kentish Town, then by the end of the LMS, during which period a mechanical coaling and ash plants had been provided, Cricklewood had the code 14A; this it retained until 9th September 1963, when it became 14B, that designation serving until closure on 14th December 1964. The sheds were both re-roofed in 1949 which gave them another fifteen years useful operation. Diesels continued to visit the shed for fuelling, though it had an increasing air of dereliction; demolition took place during May 1969 and Cricklewood shed was no more; the site was cleared and reused for a Royal Mail depot. However, study of Google Earth, Street View, of June 2016, revealed that the postal building had been removed and the cleared area was again being redeveloped – for what purpose is unknown.

Two condenser-fitted Johnson 3Fs – Nos.47216 and 47214 – stand near the ash plant on 31st May 1958, their day's work finished perhaps? When BR came into being, Cricklewood had over thirty of these former Midland Railway 0-6-0Ts allocated but by the date of this image less than half a dozen remained at 14A; these two were withdrawn during August and May 1959 respectively bringing the total down again. *C.J.B. Sanderson (ARPT).*

Cricklewood – What was on shed Saturday 19th April 1952:
40025, 40932, 41077, 42237, 42763, 42839, 43031, 43120, 43121, 43261, 43901, 43907, 43934, 43935, 44028, 44259, 44298, 44304, 44465, 45061, 47203, 47207, 47212, 47214, 47215, 47218, 47220, 47221, 47224, 47225, 47240, 47248, 47251, 47434, 47435, 48062, 48356, 48365, 48410, 48415, 58161, 58184, 58234, 58235   Total: 44.

Cricklewood – What was on shed Sunday 20th March 1955:
40021, 40023, 40024, 40025, 40030, 40119, 41048, 41712, 41826, 42237, 42756, 42839, 42855, 43031, 43118, 43120, 43121, 43244, 43261, 43307, 43440, 43901, 43934, 44029, 44228, 44259, 44297, 44529, 44530, 44545, 44563, 44581, 44774, 44777, 45059, 45335, 45575, 45615, 47203, 47207, 47209, 47210, 47211, 47215, 47216, 47220, 47221, 47224, 47226, 47240, 47248, 47251, 47433, 47434, 47435, 47554, 47974, 48062, 48132, 48150, 48163, 48198, 48219, 48305, 48360, 48365, 48367, 48376, 48410, 48414, 48415, 48461, 48541, 48617, 48681, 48692, 48750, 92018, 92019, 12064, 12065, 12066, 12068, 13022, 13024   Total: 85.

(top) Beyer-Garratt 2-6-0+0-6-2s have been running into Cricklewood since they were introduced by the LMS in 1927 but it was in 1930 when the 'production' batch was put into traffic that the engines became daily visitors to Cricklewood. This is No.47981 stabled for the weekend on Sunday 4th July 1954. *(centre)* A near broadside of the Garratt during that weekend at 14A in July 1954; the big engine was stabled near the coaling plant at the northern end of the shed yard, stabling roads had been established to take an overflow of engines from the two roundhouses but for the Garratt this was the only place to stable. No.47981 spent its whole life allocated to Toton and was withdrawn in November 1956. *Both F.W. Hampson (ARPT)*. *(bottom)* Another month, another Garratt: No.47970 on 15th August 1954. This unsightly specimen worked all of its life from Toton and was one of the early casualties being withdrawn in July 1955. *C.W. Allen (ARPT)*.

(above) We've done the Garratts now let's look at the Crostis': No.92027 dumped in the siding alongside the advertising hoarding' on Edgware Road 27th June 1960. There were so many hoardings it was difficult to see the shed yard so leaving the 9F there would not draw attention to its plight. This particular 9F was stored here from April 1959 to August 1960; it was converted in October. *Howard Foster. (below)* Here is a working example, No.92025, on the shed yard on 26th February 1956. The smoke deflector over the side chimney was a recent fitting to help eliminate the ingress of smoke into the cab. A feature rarely commented on with these ten Crosti 9Fs is the handrail below the cab window on this side of the engine, and the associated footboard/rail below the side sheet to enable access to the running plate behind the side chimney. *C.J.B. Sanderson (ARPT).*

Cricklewood – What was on shed Sunday 24th May 1959:
40021, 40023, 42329, 42629, 43019, 43031, 43118, 43120, 43905, 43971, 44029, 44043, 44051, 44228, 44259, 44381, 44529, 44532, 44542, 44812, 44941, 45059, 45062, 45238, 47210, 47211, 47212, 47216, 47226, 47248, 47433, 47434, 47435, 48142, 48180, 48301, 48313, 48324, 48367, 48386, 48538, 48616, 48678, 58131, 73048, 75055, 80143, 92019, 92027, 92052, 92054, 92086, 92100, 92123, 92124, 92126, 92138, 92154, 92159, 92163, 12067, 12068, 12069, 12072, D3023, 13024, 13179, D3181, 13249, D570   Total: 70.

Cricklewood – What was on shed Sunday 25th February 1962:
42086, 42178, 42325, 42329, 42686, 43019, 43031, 43118, 43808, 43947, 44051, 44259, 44297, 44441, 44529, 44581, 44774, 44816, 44846, 45274, 45668, 47211, 47248, 47432, 47433, 47434, 47435, 47642, 48117, 48141, 48143, 48301, 48304, 48306, 48313, 48378, 48625, 92018, 92026, 92106, 92108, 92124, 92126, 92154, 12058, 12065, 12069, 13305, D3181, D5087, D5090   Total: 50.

Nottingham based 'Jubilee' No.45650 BLAKE was a natural choice for this special working (M60) because it had just completed a Heavy Intermediate overhaul and was in pristine mechanical if not external condition. The date was 31st May 1958, a Saturday, and the Raleigh 1958 Works Outing was the occasion. It is by now late afternoon and the 6P is turned and serviced ready for the journey back to Nottingham which would take part during the latter period of the evening; it is quite possible that more than one such special excursion was run. Another 'Jubilee' is stabled alongside our subject whilst resident tank engines are put away for the weekend. *C.J.B. Sanderson (ARPT).*

Caprotti Standard 5 No.73142 stabled in the same position on 26th March 1961. The Rowsley based 4-6-0 had just clocked up 170,000 miles 'since new' in December 1956 – about 40,000 a year! What it went on to achieve is unknown because from 1963 onwards such records were not uniformly kept and by the time it was withdrawn in April 1968, they certainly were not kept anywhere. Starting life at Leicester (*see* also Kentish Town), the '5' transferred to Derby in January 1959 but later that year reallocated to Rowsley along with sisters 73135 to 73144, just like that! The home of the Caprotti Standard 5s beckoned and during 1964 all of those engines migrated to Patricroft, our subject here arriving in May to join the earlier arrivals 73125 to 73134, and meet fellow immigrants 73157 to 73160, 73163, 73165, and eleven other engines from the earlier batches which had ended up there. The Caprotti engines were quite successful on BR metals and popular with footplate men and fitters, even though their external condition may contradict that fact. *C.J.B. Sanderson (ARPT).*

Cricklewood – What was on shed Sunday 28th April 1963:
42070, 42086, 42090, 42092, 42680, 44529, 44667, 44777, 44821, 44826, 45217, 45277, 45450, 45561, 45568, 46143, 46163, 47202, 47432, 47434, 47435, 47437, 47543, 47611, 48517, 73157, 73158, 76035, 76037, 76038, 76039, 76040, 76041, 76043, 76048, 76085, 76086, 76088, 76089, 92009, 12058, 12063, 12069, D53, D110, D135, D151, D3024, D3179, D3249, D3305, D3306, D3573, 3773, D4117, D4131, D5085, D5086, D5087, D5089, D5188, D5379, D5386, D5387, D5388, D5390, D5396, D5398, D5400, D5403, D5408, D5414, D5415   Total: 73.

Two of the Metro-Vick Co-Bos (Bo-Co in this case) – D5714 and D5715 – stable outside Cricklewood roundhouse circa 1959 during the period when the class were employed on, amongst other duties, the *CONDOR* overnight express freight service between London and Glasgow. The initial service was launched on Monday 16th March 1959, the Up train departing Glasgow at 7.50 p.m., with two of these diesel locomotives employed; a Down working left Hendon at a similar time. By the end of the year so much had gone wrong with the diesels that steam locomotives (Stanier Cl.5s) were working the named train. This view therefore is probably from the period in 1959 when the Co-Bos were *actually* working. The connecting doors appear to have been welded-up but perhaps they were so well fitted that appearances deceive? However, something has been applied to seal the gaps and eradicate those annoying draughts. The front windows are still wrap-around type which dates these locomotives to that period when they were new. Note the wrong-facing BR crest adorning the side of the locomotive – it seems that everything which could go wrong with this class, did! *Gordon Turner/GD/ARPT.*

Whereas the Western Lines of the LMR put all their eggs into the electrification basket, the Midland Lines of the region invested in diesel locomotives. Amongst those chosen to work the mixed traffic on the southern section of the route were these BRC&W Type 2 Bo-Bo diesel electrics which, as things turned out, were quite successful. Ranged here outside Cricklewood roundhouse on 23rd September 1962 were D5386, D5397 and others with deliveries continuing. 14A was allocated a batch of these locomotives ranging from D5379 to D5415 which all came new from the makers in 1962 between the end of March and the beginning of October. On 30th January 1965 Cricklewood lost its locomotive allocation as such when the newly created London Division of the LMR was created (the LMR engine sheds went into a state flux during this period when numerous divisions, lines, and other entities were created but these all went by the board when TOPS was introduced and the depots regained their recognition and identities) but D5386 proudly displays a 14A shed plate meantime. *N.W. Skinner (ARPT).*

No.92122 from Wellingborough on 22ⁿᵈ September 1957. Cricklewood was to get a small allocation of 9Fs of its own – 92110, 92111, and 92112 – from November 1956 to May 1959, joined towards the end of that stint by No.92119. *Norman Preedy*.

Ivatt Cl.2 No.41208 started life at Kentish Town but was transferred to Cricklewood in November 1949. Here is the 2-6-2T on 6ᵗʰ August 1950 still sporting its LMS logo although only the middle section is visible through the dirt. It had been renumbered just two months previously on 10ᵗʰ June, on shed, but the BR emblem would have to wait until the engines' next works visit. Sister No.41207 was also allocated to 14A and followed No.41208 to Bristol in June 1956 when the pair transferred to Barrow Road. *Norman Preedy*.

Cricklewood – What was on shed Tuesday 28ᵗʰ July 1964:
42086, 42090, 42092, 44717, 45059, 45207, 45215, 46156, 47435, 48116, 48195, 48368, 61387, 73066, 73069, 73159, 76035, 76041, 92124, 12067, D69,   D74,   D90,   D96,   D105, D142, D154, D155, D285, D3773, D4134, D5088, D5090, D5092, D5206, D5214, D5215, D5223, D5266, D5285, D5398, D5402, D5415, D7577, D7596   Total: 45.

CAMDEN

The first of Camden's three engine sheds was opened by the London & Birmingham Railway (LBR) on 20th June 1837. An imposing, stone built structure standing on the north side of the main line at the summit of Camden Bank, the depot was square in plan-form with two entrances at the west end; each led inside, to a row of eight turn plates, from which roads radiated to stabling stalls at the sides and in the centre. That shed was destined to last for only ten years though, as traffic requirements especially freight, meant space had to be found for an inner-London goods yard, so in 1847 the LBR's successor (July 1846), the L&NWR, provided two engine sheds. One was a conical roofed, brick roundhouse which stood north of the line, immediately by that new goods yard. It was designated as the Luggage Engine House, while on the other side of the line a massively-built brick building of five through roads was provided for the Passenger Engine House.

The roundhouse served only until 1871, being closed and devoted to other uses; for many years it was an alcoholic spirit warehouse for Messrs Gilbey, before it fell out of use. The historic structure was rescued, however, and converted into a world-renowned arts centre The Camden Roundhouse, and it continues in such use. The five road straight shed was equipped with a turntable at the east end, where a two road coaling shed adjoined the main building; at the west end a three road coke store also adjoined the main building. During various late LNWR and early LMS improvements, those two small sheds were converted for additional stabling. Also a first mechanical coaling plant and ash hoist was erected, both later replaced by more modern types, while the turntable was in time, relocated to the west end and enlarged. Finally, the original gable roof was replaced by a concrete Louvre type.

Coded 1 at the beginning of the LMS, by 1947 Camden had the designation 1B, which served through BR times, to closure to steam in September 1963 and finally to diesels in January 1966, with completion of electrification of the lines out of Euston. Camden shed was soon taken down and the site used for carriage and multiple unit stabling sidings, which exist today.

Kingmoor based 'Princess Royal' No.46200 THE PRINCESS ROYAL rubbing shoulders with the enemy in June 1962 at the south end of Camden's yard. It was this locomotive which started the Pacific revolution on the LMS in 1933 and from which we got thirty years of pure brilliance (only fifteen in my case because I'm not that old) culminating in the last two Pacifics 'Stanier' and 'Salford'. No.46200 had spent the previous winter in store at Carnforth 3rd September 1961 to 19th January 1962 but it wouldn't see another winter – at least in BR employ – as it was withdrawn 17th November 1962. Behind is an unidentified 'Royal Scot' with no regimental batch on the single line nameplate (that should easy enough to assume). To the left of the yard are the new order, English Electric Type 4 diesel-electrics D383 and D210 EMPRESS OF BRITAIN. These diesels had already taken over at Camden and the presence of these Pacifics would soon become a memory. However, within four years of this scene being captured on film the order would change again as electric traction would take over the main line passenger services in and out of Euston. *S.C. Crook (ARPT)*.

A visit to the shed on Saturday 12th July 1952 found the following:
44712, 44758, 44897, 45525, 45526, 45532, 45555, 45587, 45632, 45676, 45680, 45689, 45701, 45708, 45712, 45742, 46111, 46137, 46147, 46154, 46155, 46161, 46166, 46168, 46204, 46227, 46232, 46233, 46252, 46255, 46257, 47467.   Total 32.

46209 PRINCESS BEATRICE, minus nameplates, and sister 46206 PRINCESS MARIE LOUISE, probably similarly de-named, languish at the south end of the shed yard on Saturday 22nd September 1962. The Pacifics had just started a bout of storage, their last as things transpired, on the previous Thursday 13th. No.46206 would be condemned on 3rd November whereas sister '09' was withdrawn during the week following this scene being recorded. Perhaps more significantly steam working at Camden had just finished, these storage episodes were created simply to get the engines out of traffic prior to moving them to Crewe for scrapping. Both of these engines had spent periods in store at various times throughout their lives. Coincidentally, they had both been transferred away from London at the outbreak of WW2 and went to Longsight where they were tallowed down for three weeks – 11th September to 2nd October 1939 – before returning to traffic. No.46206 was put into store at Rugby twice in 1961 thus: 12th March to 3rd July after which it went to Crewe for the summer season; then on 10th September 1961 to 21st January 1962 when Camden called. This latest period out of traffic was as a result of the ending of the summer timetable and the continuing delivery of main-line diesel locomotives to handle the Anglo-Scottish expresses. No.46209 was a Crewe North engine when stored from 12th March to 16th June 1961. Again high seasonal traffic levels saw the 'Princess' enjoy three ,months back in the limelight but the winter approached and 46209 was back in grease and cloth from 6th September 1961 to 25th January 1962. Four days after her sister transferred to 1B, 46209 followed. Camden shed never did have the capacity to store too many locomotives and these two were each taking up valuable siding space in a depot which had just four short sidings but by then it didn't really matter as the diesels didn't require much shed time. *N.W.Skinner (ARPT).*

Apologies for even thinking about including this illustration of Turbomotive No.6202 but the historical significance of this image was overwhelming in that it presents the tragic Pacific in all its former glory on the Camden turntable in 1937. The turntable was as old as the 'Princess' and had been installed as one of the major improvements carried out at Camden by the LMS during the 1930s in order to service the forthcoming Pacifics. *Walter I.O. Moffat (ARPT).*

Camden – What was on shed Saturday 10th January 1953:

45021, 45048, 45187, 45250, 45331, 45344, 45514, 45522, 45532, 45545, 45586, 45601, 45613, 45644, 45676, 45738, 46112, 46122, 46124, 46141, 46147, 46163, 46168, 46208, 46229, 46235, 46238, 46239, 12023   Total: 29.

Camden – What was on shed Sunday 19th December 1954:

42886, 44678, 45333, 45372, 45441, 45523, 45531, 45532, 45535, 45545, 45595, 45624, 45647, 45669, 45686, 45688, 45726, 45735, 46101, 46123, 46126, 46135, 46139, 46146, 46148, 46157, 46166, 46169, 46201, 46226, 46237, 46239, 46244, 46254, 46256, 46257, 47354, 47356, 47358, 47359, 47467, 47667, 47668, 70031, 70045, 70047, 73070, 12033   Total: 48.

'Princess' No.46205 PRINCESS VICTORIA rests on Camden shed yard in August 1961 ready for another northbound working. Recently out of storage at Willesden (26th March to 7th July 1961), our subject was only in traffic for a couple of months before it was taken back to 1A and put into mothballs on 17th September. All was well until the week ending Saturday 25th November 1961 when withdrawal took place and another of the LMR's finest was condemned to the cutting up shop at Crewe works, the sixth 'Princess Royal' that year. *A.R.Thompson (ARPT)*.

Edge Hill 'Rebuilt Patriot' No.45531 SIR FREDERICK HARRISON with the headboard for *THE SHAMROCK* express is ready to work back to Liverpool on Monday afternoon 19th May 1958. The 7P is fully coaled and is waiting ready for the off whatever time that was to back down to Euston. Note the massive bulk of the ash plant behind, which has an appendage not normally seen on other similar plants; the skip hoist is fully enclosed to stop the contents blowing over the neighbouring residential properties and causing a nuisance. Smoke inspectors and their like were always patrolling this depot waiting for the chance to slap a notice on BR for smoke nuisance too! Now deciding what is or isn't a smoke nuisance offence is surely in the eye of the beholder as it cannot be scientifically measured without proper equipment. So, were all those summonses issued to BR by local Town Halls really just a chance to extract some money from the public purse to put into another? *C.J.B. Sanderson (ARPT)*.

Back to that turntable at the north end of the shed yard but we have come forward in time to 19ᵗʰ May 1958 to watch 'Jubilee' No.45592 INDORE revolve around some 180 degrees ready to work another train to the north. The 6P was one of the half dozen or so resident 'Jubilees' although none of them were ever at Camden that long and were forever changing through transfer between sheds. *C.J.B. Sanderson (ARPT)*.

No.45632 TONGA takes to the table on that nineteenth day of May in 1958 after delivering an express from Manchester (London Road) to Euston. A Longsight engine at the time, the 6P was about to transfer to Chester but was to be reallocated to Camden during the following April, its first and only residency at 1B. *C.J.B. Sanderson (ARPT)*.

Standing at the north end of the shed, resident No.45669 FISHER, was looking extremely smart on that afternoon in May 1958 but it wasn't down to a works visit although the 6P had been for Heavy Intermediate more than a year beforehand. It was all down to graft and elbow grease applied by the cleaners employed here. The Camden 'Jubilees' were used mainly for the Birmingham workings although those same trains could have a 'Duchess' in charge sometimes. *C.J.B. Sanderson (ARPT)*.

(opposite top) No.46134 THE CHESHIRE REGIMENT looks rather smart in this Monday 19th May 1958 afternoon scene at Camden where an equally smart sister engine is stabled alongside. The Crewe based 7P (were any of them based anywhere for any length of time excepting perhaps the Scottish contingent?) had just completed a Heavy General overhaul at Crewe so that accounts for the cleanliness. From Nationalisation up to its withdrawal in late 1962, this particular 'Scot' had a dozen transfers. However, during its life it clocked up an impressive two-million miles plus in revenue earning service. Now, not wanting to cause any panic, but what about those cylinders in the four-foot containing oxygen and acetylene; I don't remember reading anything about Camden and an explosion but the shed did close rather quickly! *C.J.B. Sanderson (ARPT).*

(opposite centre) Longsight's No.46160 QUEEN VICTORIA'S RIFLEMAN on the ash pit at Camden 19th May 1958. On the ground, in the six-foot, lies the two main pieces of a water crane with the column furthest away and the swinging arm (though not any more) nearest. The appliance appears to have come from that bunded space near the tender, just before the lighting tower. No doubt removed to make reservation for the forthcoming diesels. *C.J.B. Sanderson (ARPT).*

(opposite bottom) Longsight shed was certainly represented at Camden on this afternoon in May 1958. This is No.46169 THE BOY SCOUT on the north yard wearing one of those dodgy BR crests. Behind is 'Jubilee' No.45595 making its slow way through the five-road shed towards the south end to be ready for departure to Euston whenever that event arose! The throughput at this shed was quite phenomenal but the straight forward layout finalised by the LMS in 1935 enabled the shed to function continually as a moving entity with locomotives arriving from Euston, being serviced – turned, coaled, fire cleaned, watered, and lubricated – and then departing back to the terminus. It even had a two-road repair shop for those niggly jobs which didn't require a trip to Willesden or Crewe works! *C.J.B. Sanderson (ARPT).*

Note the coal arranged in No.46241's tender! It has been placed in to get the maximum amount in the bunker because CITY OF EDINBURGH has got a lot of hard work to do getting *THE CALEDONIAN* up to Carlisle where an equally prepared 'Duchess' will be waiting to take over for the run to Glasgow. The train was inaugurated on 17th June 1957 with a 0830 departure from Glasgow (Central) and a 1615 departure from London (Euston). The 401 mile journey was covered in six hours and forty minutes averaging 60.2 m.p.h. The train was just a Monday to Friday operation initially but in the summer 1958 timetable (9th June) it was to be duplicated to give a morning departure from London and an afternoon departure from Glasgow. This Pacific was waiting to reverse down to the terminus on Monday 19th May 1958 to work the then daily Down train. *C.J.B. Sanderson (ARPT).*

Camden – What was on shed Sunday 4th March 1956:
44682, 44711, 44860, 45340, 45374, 45381, 45430, 45523, 45526, 45528, 45555, 45592, 45601, 45606, 45672, 45735, 45740, 46106, 46126, 46140, 46142, 46149, 46153, 46156, 46159, 46162, 46226, 46229, 46236, 46237, 46239, 46245, 46250, 46253, 46257, 47529, 47669, 70047, 71000, 12033   Total: 40.

Camden – What was on shed Sunday 25th February 1962:
41239, 44866, 45288, 45736, 46209, 46240, 46246, 46254, D2,   D4,   D223, D228, D229, D232, D269, D288, D290, D304, D315, D316, D327, D332, D340, D370, D372, D375, D377, D378, D3850, D8003, D8037   Total: 31.

Possibly the worst engine-tender combination ever, or was it an 8F with a Fowler tender, or the 'Crab' which only ever had the Fowler tender anyway, so couldn't really be compared. 'Jubilee' No.45722 DEFENCE was coupled to this tender (No.4497) from July 1956 to March 1959; it didn't end there though because another Fowler tender was waiting (No.3187) to be attached after a Light Intermediate overhaul. In February 1960 a Stanier tender (No.10787) was coupled to the 'Jubilee' during a Casual Light repair, the Fowler nightmare, which started in July 1948 with No.4484 from a 'Baby Scot', was over. It had run nearly half a million miles dragging one of those ugly bugs! *C.J.B. Sanderson (ARPT)*.

Another Longsight 'Jubilee' No.45595 SOUTHERN RHODESIA, and another of those dreadful Fowler tender couplings. No.45595 was about to get rid of the tender (September at a Light Intermediate) after twenty-two years of attachment to three of them. I don't know if a clean was thrown in with the LI but such an event would not go amiss. *C.J.B. Sanderson (ARPT)*.

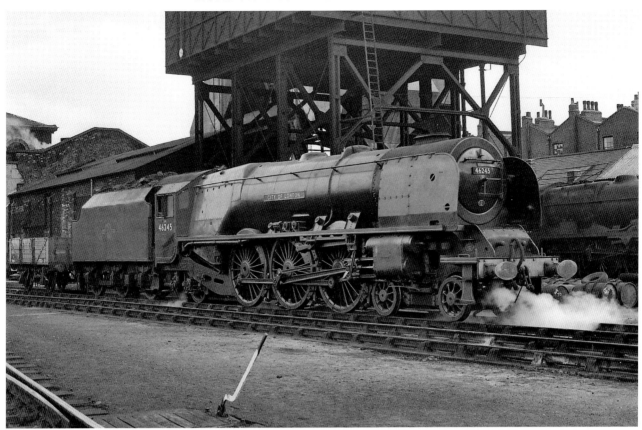

It had to be the only shed for this 'Duchess' – No.46245 CITY OF LONDON stables beneath the depot's water tower and coaling plant on 19th May 1958. During the previous January this engine was exhibited at Euston station for the BR Board to inspect the new maroon livery which was to be worn eventually by sixteen members of the class. *C.J.B. Sanderson (ARPT)*.

Camden's shed pilot, 3F 0-6-0T No.47310 on 19th May 1958. Besides this tank, 1B also possessed another eleven of the class virtually up to closure but they don't show up much in the 'engines on shed' lists because they were nearly always out working the carriage sidings, Euston station, and whatever else was required of them. Note the new heating hose for the carriage work – even now in the late spring the overnight sleepers needed warming before the passengers arrived. No.47310 was a recent arrival at Camden, an orphan from Devons Road dieselisation. It didn't stay long and it was off to Bescot by late 1959. *C.J.B. Sanderson (ARPT)*.

CITY OF STOKE-ON-TRENT is made ready for its next northbound working on 7th May 1960. Now this 'Duchess' was, at the time that this image was captured, wearing a maroon livery with the old lining style used on the green livery. Things were about to change however as No.46254 was soon to visit Crewe where it would receive the revised second maroon livery with black and yellow – LMS style – lining close to the edge of the panels. This Pacific had been given a fully lined green livery in April 1957, and then, in September 1958 it was given this livery. Still looks magnificent no matter which livery was worn. On the extreme right one of Camden's recent English Electric Type 1 acquisitions, D8037, is working the shed yard. *Norman Preedy.*

This 'Brit' is slightly special and no it's not because of that lack of a name, or the exceedingly filthy tender with the mountain of coal. It's that little nameplate holder on the cab side; it's actually got a nameplate inserted! The Holyhead based Pacific was soon to carry the name ANZAC but for the moment it's really carrying the drivers' name. Oh, not forgetting another temporary name adorning the 7P – THE IRISH MAIL headboard. Now just what is going on in that pit? *C.J.B. Sanderson (ARPT).*

Maligned, rubbished, the butt of jokes, a financial disaster. It was all those things and more to BR. They just didn't get it right and it was left to a bunch of enthusiasts to put the record straight or rather put the locomotive straight! The one and only BR Standard 8P No.71000 DUKE OF GLOUCESTER runs onto the south yard after visiting the turntable and coaler. Now it's time to clean out the ash pan. The date!? Of course it's 18th May 1958. In typical 5A fashion, the Pacific is looking rather filthy. *C.J.B. Sanderson (ARPT).*

Any room at the inn!? The disposition at the south end of Camden shed yard circa June 1962 with 'Duchess' No.46245 CITY OF LONDON ready to work off shed from the ash wagon road. The neighbours are close but as I always ask myself when people living near airports forever complain about noise. Who was there first? The Pacific looks tremendous whilst the very noisy neighbours look on from the stabling roads. *Book Law Publications.*

Camden – What was on shed Sunday 28th April 1963:
46225, 46228, 46229, 46239, 46240, 46251, 46252, D213, D226, D228, D229, D231, D268, D289, D292, D311, D312, D325, D326, D328, D329, D340, D369, D370, D376, D378, D3015, D3017, D3849, D3850, D5019, D8037, D8039   Total: 33.

KENTISH TOWN

Midland Railway services commenced running into London in 1859, via Bedford and the Great Northern Railway (GNR), from Hitchin, to Kings Cross. Between 1867/8, however, the MR completed its own route into the Capital with a terminus at the iconic St. Pancras. A locomotive shed was erected a few miles north, on the east side of the main line; two adjoining square plan-form roundhouses, numbered 1 and 2, with attendant repair shop and coaling stage. As with all other railways serving London the MR eventually found it necessary to increase track capacity, so roundhouse one and the repair shop were removed in 1898 and new lines built over their sites, while two more square turntable sheds were added, all adjoining but *en echelon* along a northwest to southeast axis. Roundhouse 2 became No.1 and the others, Nos. 2 and 3; finally a new repair shop and double-sided coal stage completed the depot's rearrangements in 1899.

The LMS carried out improvements at the end of the 1930s, with a mechanical coaling plant and ash towers, while roundhouses 2 and 3 were partly de-roofed with what remained being renewed. By the latter 1950s, however, No.3 had become unsafe and was closed off with barrier ropes while at about the same time, No.1 received a brand-new roof of concrete and glass. Kentish Town's prime duties concerned mainline passenger and the very busy suburban services out to St. Albans and Bedford. In fact roundhouse 1 was always called the Metro shed because it invariably housed the many tank engines used on those inner workings. Coded 16 by the MR the depot became 14B in LMS days and that continued under BR. Dieselisation of the MR main line came relatively early, with the result that Kentish Town shed closed in April 1963. That was not the end though as the much modified buildings serve today in commercial use, latterly by the civil engineering firm Murphy.

Inside No.1 shed, facing east towards the water softener, which is visible outside on the left of the image. The date is 8th May 1955, a Sunday, and gathered around the turntable (this is no longer a 46ft diameter appliance) from left are: Stanier Cl.3 No.40119, Fowler Cl.3 No.40035, Fowler Cl.3 No.40034, BR Std.Cl.4 No.80048, and Stanier Cl.3 No.40166, with a 3F 0-6-0T behind. Diesel multiple units have yet to make an impact in this part of the world so this lot have got at least another summer of work before redundancies start. The first to go from this gathering was Cl.3 No.40166 which was reallocated to Liverpool's Bank Hall shed during the following November. It was from that date approximately when it all started to go wrong. Finally, what on earth has fallen from the roof to bend that guard rail on the table? *F.W.Hampson (ARPT)*.

A visit to Kentish Town on Saturday 12th July 1952 found: 40021, 40032, 40033, 40035, 40036, 40037, 40038, 40092, 40114, 40119, 40142, 40167, 40547, 40900, 41061, 41077, 41083, 41091, 41249, 41664, 41671, 41713, 41724, 42138, 42139, 42237, 42300, 42341, 42839, 43033, 44052, 44210, 44563, 44600, 44658, 44665, 44754, 45088, 45277, 45279, 45285, 45342, 45569, 45585, 45611, 45615, 45616, 45620, 45627, 45655, 47200, 47202, 47204, 47205, 47215, 47229, 47240, 47241, 47243, 47244, 47260, 47283, 47428, 47437, 47644, 47645, 58131, 58132, 58158, 58216, 58229
Total: 71.

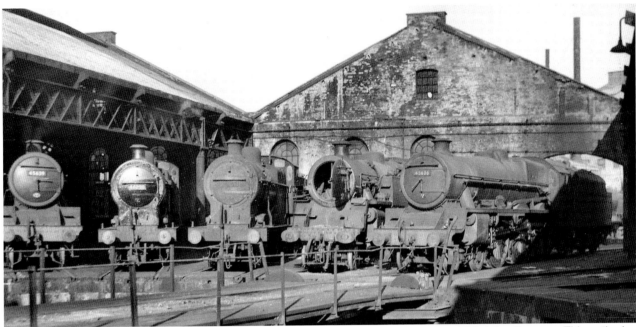

No.2 shed same Sunday, 8th May 1955! The photographer is now facing south-east and it is late afternoon. This gathering includes two 'Jubilees' Nos.45636 UGANDA (Nottingham) and 45639 RALEIGH (Leeds Holbeck) [one would have expected the homes of the 6Ps to have been the other way round!], a pair of 4Fs with only resident No.44298 identifiable on the left, and another resident, BR Std. Cl.4 No.80045. *F.W.Hampson (ARPT)*.

The LMS No.1 type coaler, which had a 300-ton capacity divided over four bunkers, was erected during the dark days at the beginning of WW2. What the locals must have thought with that going up and German bombs dropping all over the city, goodness only knows. The Cl.3 tank, No.40031 was one of fourteen of the class allocated during BR days – they were all over north London like a rash with Willesden and Cricklewood contributing too. For working over the Metropolitan lines, Nos.40021 to 40040 were fitted with condenser apparatus. Note also the push-pull gear, outside steam pipes, and wider chimney; the last two features being retro-fitted to make the class perform better. We have no date for this image but at least the 2-6-2T has the correct version of BR crest so it must have been post October 1958. *V.Wake (ARPT)*.

A visit on 7th October 1959 found withdrawn Cl.3 No.40027, one of those tanks which didn't have the alterations to bring the steam pipes outside, looking rather poorly. The cull had started and Kentish Town was determined to get rid of these six-coupled tanks first but Willesden was also in the race along with half a dozen other engine sheds. The possible reason for this 2-6-2Ts demise is a bent component in the valve gear perhaps! Shed plate removed, number plate still attached but nobody at 14B cared about the latter, just the former. Behind, Stanier 3MT No.40172 had also been condemned. Like I said, the cull had begun! *N.W.Skinner (ARPT).*

'Jubilee' No.45579 PUNJAB waits for coal at Kentish Town on 19th May 1958. This 6P had been at 14B since August 1952, initially 'on loan' and then with a permanence two weeks into September. The transfer was part of a larger mass transfer involving sixteen 'Jubilee' from Scottish Region to English sheds, and a similar number from English sheds to Scottish Region, after which things settled down, to a point. Shopping was considered before the England based engines went north because St Rollox works didn't hold stocks of both boiler types used by the class. However, those former ScR. engines now in England initially had to make the trek to Glasgow for shopping. Hence the reason why No.45579 still has the large style numerals on its cab side six years after transferring from Polmadie to 14B. The 6P had only been given one Heavy General during that period (June and July 1955) and that is when the large figures were applied. So, where did it receive that new BR crest on the tender? *C.J.B. Sanderson (ARPT).*

3F No.47202 stabled in the yard next to the main line on 28th October 1962. When most of the locomotives around her had already been withdrawn or were about to be, it seems surprising that this 0-6-0T was reallocated to Cricklewood – where it all started for the Johnson tank – from where in 1963 a transfer to Gorton saw the old lady get a new lease of time serving various depots in the Greater Manchester area, including a stint at Horwich works which then took the 3F to a December 1966 withdrawal. *Howard Foster.*

Is this the end? It is Sunday 28th October 1962 and BR Std. Cl.2 No.84029 is dumped at Kentish Town looking as though its withdrawn but that pane of glass would be easily fixed and during the following January the 2-6-2T was transferred to Wellingborough on the 15th; then within days of arriving there, it was moved on to Leicester where on 18th March 1963 it was put back into storage (perhaps the glass never was changed) where it remained until 6th April 1964. The Cl.2 was withdrawn on 13th June 1964 so what happened to it between those

last two dates? Nothing! It seems all so surreal now. No.84029 was just five years old when this image was recorded; sisters 84005 and 84008 followed the same path and the bunker of one of them is just in picture here. Reallocated from Neasden to Kentish Town during July 1962, the tank engines had absolutely no prospect of any work at 14B hence their forced inactivity; even the vacuum controlled push-pull gear has been removed. As a mark of defiance perhaps, No.84029 retains the dodgy BR crest which it would eventually take to a scrapyard in the West Midlands. For the record, this was the last steam locomotive built at Darlington works. *Howard Foster.*

Kentish Town – What was on shed Sunday 4th March 1956:
40021, 40029, 40031, 40033, 40034, 40036, 40092, 40111, 40119, 40142, 40160, 40167, 40172, 41068, 41191, 42237, 42300, 42682, 42685, 42761, 42795, 42823, 43846, 43919, 43934, 44052, 44143, 44243, 44298, 44563, 44809, 44818, 44819, 44825, 44830, 44839, 45253, 45279, 45285, 45554, 45562, 45564, 45566, 45568, 45573, 45585, 45589, 45611, 45614, 45616, 45641, 45655, 45667, 47202, 47205, 47209, 47212, 47229, 47241, 47243, 47283, 47437, 47642, 47645, 48748, 58131, 58215, 73011, 12063, 12068, 13023   Total: 71.

Kentish Town – What was on shed Sunday 19th January 1958:
40021, 40027, 40029, 40032, 40033, 40034, 40035, 40036, 40038, 40040, 40092, 40100, 40167, 40172, 40413, 40420, 40421, 40452, 40534, 40536, 40543, 40567, 40580, 40925, 41071, 41100, 41114, 42157, 42237, 42453, 42587, 42682, 42685, 44243, 44270, 44298, 44516, 44531, 44755, 44777, 44821, 44845, 45285, 45575, 45608, 45612, 45615, 45616, 45636, 45649, 45656, 46110, 46116, 46152, 47202, 47204, 47205, 47209, 47213, 47226, 47229, 47241, 47246, 47260, 47283, 47437, 47644, 47645, 58131, 73171, 12072   Total: 71.

Kentish Town – What was on shed Sunday 25th February 1962:
40022, 40024, 40031, 40111, 40119, 40203, 42279, 42334, 42336, 42342, 42595, 42610, 43964, 44210, 44243, 44532, 44817, 44822, 45277, 45614, 45622, 45712, 46112, 47202, 47213, 47223, 47261, 47283, 47437, 47442, 47449, 47485, 47502, 47554, 47611, 47645, 70053, 70054, D69   Total: 39.

Kentish Town – What was on shed Sunday 28th April 1963:
12064, D3180, D3869, D5092, D5382, D5385, D5393, D5402, D5405, D5406, D5409, D5413   Total: 12.

KING'S CROSS

Probably the most famous of London engine sheds, King's Cross for most of its life, carried the appellation 'Top Shed'. It was home to the premier express passenger engines of the GNR, the LNER and finally, BR Eastern Region. Denizens like the Gresley and Peppercorn Pacifics, and the men working them, became famous for their numerous speed achievements, a state of affairs that continued right up to the coming of the diesels.

The first building put up for the GNR and opened in 1851, was of a rare fan type layout with points leading to the crescent-shaped depot's twenty-five stabling roads; a turntable stood in the yard, as did a coaling stage. In 1859 to serve MR engines working into King's Cross station, the GNR built a circular roundhouse with its own coaling stage and three years later, an eight road, through shed was put up in front of the crescent. All eight roads passed through, into the rear building which then became a repair shop for locomotives and carriage stock; later the carriage repair section reverted to locomotive use, becoming known as the 'Met' shed, where were stabled the many tank engines working the GN's suburban services. The LNER provided a huge mechanical coal tower, wet ash pits and later, overhead watering facilities at what became known as the 'Back Pits.' They covered the site of the MR roundhouse which since MR engines left Kings Cross, had been used by the GNR and LNER for locomotive stabling, before being demolished in 1931/2. The straight shed suffered bomb damage in 1940, which was temporarily repaired at the time, leaving BR the job of renewing the roof in 1949; the Met shed roof was also replaced at the same time.

Coded KX by the LNER, Top Shed became 34A in BR times. Diesels arrived at the end of the 1950s, but steam's rear-guard action continued in dwindling fashion, until closure of Top Shed on 17th June 1963. The site was cleared and today hosts tracks of the High Speed Railway from the Channel Tunnel into St. Pancras, commercial and industrial buildings, and some open areas still to come under major redevelopment.

The most common pictures taken at King's Cross shed were those of numerous and varied line-ups of locomotives, mostly Pacifics, outside the eight road building – invariably awe-inspiring sights! So general panoramas of the depot are scarce, hence we start our look at 34A with this scene from Sunday 14th April 1957. From left we see smoke coming from the area around the coaling tower, then the grab crane which serviced the ever-busy ash pits. The first identified locomotive is V2 No.60871, visiting from Doncaster. Then comes the eight-road main shed with what looks like among others, three Thompson A1 and two A3 Pacifics waiting for their next duties; the high-roofed building behind that, with two longitudinal vents is part of the original 1851 crescent shed, covering the depot's repair shop. Next we have WD 2-8-0 No.90106 from New England. Right again, barely visible behind the 'Back Pits' with the overhead water facility, is the lowered roof of the north end of the crescent – the so-called Met Shed. At the Back Pits we can just see Kings Cross shed's steam breakdown crane. Finally, five N2 six-coupled tank 0-6-2T locomotives are lined up – from left to right: No.69534 from Hatfield, Nos.69535, 69592, 69539 and 69538 respectively, all 34A. *F.W. Hampson (ARPT)*.

King's Cross – What was on shed Saturday 10th January 1953:

60008, 60010, 60014, 60022, 60028, 60029, 60039, 60056, 60067, 60109, 60125, 60127, 60144, 60155, 60520, 60826, 60853, 60849, 60862, 60869, 60881, 60909, 60911, 60913, 60948, 60956, 61087, 61821, 64679, 67720, 67756, 67757, 67799, 68771, 68799, 68802, 68805, 68822, 68838, 68862, 68874, 68881, 69490, 69492, 69512, 69524, 69528, 69536, 69540, 69541, 69543, 69545, 69549, 69571, 69575, 69577, 69583, 69593, 69638, 69640, 69689, 69692   Total: 62.

A stranger in the camp! Much discussion on Wednesday 5th May 1948 after ex-LMS Princess Coronation No.46236 CITY OF BRADFORD has just arrived at Kings Cross shed from its home depot at Camden. In its original BR livery of black, lined-out in straw, with the smokebox shaped as necessary for its previous streamlined form, No.46236 is seen coupled to the ex-North Eastern Railway Dynamometer Car for the engine's part in the Locomotive Exchange Trials over the East Coast Main Line. Next day the Pacific would run from King's Cross to Leeds, returning from there on Friday 7th May. The engine had already performed on its home turf between Euston and Carlisle, with *THE ROYAL SCOT* (22nd and 23rd April) and next would be tested on the Waterloo – Exeter line (25th and 26th May), with final runs between Paddington and Plymouth and return (24th and 25th June). Overall it seems Mr Stanier's Pacific performed well during the exchanges but apparently there was talk (!) that the London Midland Region crews quietly sacrificed time from the schedules, in order to present reasonable figures for coal consumption. Your admittedly, GWR-favouring author will stay neutral and make no comment! *J.W. Armstrong (ARPT).*

At just twenty months old and still carrying the original sheet-metal chimney, Peppercorn A1 No.60133 POMMERN waits at King's Cross before taking *THE WEST RIDING* express back to the north of England. The locomotive emerged from Darlington in October 1948, being allocated initially to Grantham but transferring to Copley Hill shed on 4th June 1950, and it now carries that depot's 37B shed plate. Destined to last for less than seventeen years, No.60133 would relocate to Ardsley in June 1964, to be taken out of service exactly a year later. When first instituted in 1937 *THE WEST RIDING LIMITED* express was one of the LNER's three streamlined trains (less the observation car), aimed at business people with interests in London and the major West Riding towns, Wakefield, Leeds and Bradford. Suspended during WW2 the service was re-introduced in 1949, initially with streamlined stock which was later replaced by ordinary carriages; the train ceased to run about 1963. Like the majority of East Coast Pacifics the engine was named for a famous racehorse: the flesh and blood Pommern won the 1915 English Triple Crown (2000 Guineas, Derby and St. Leger), before being retired the next year. *C.J.B. Sanderson (ARPT).*

In most enthusiasts' eyes this is what King's Cross shed was all about! Pacifics lined-up, being prepared for their next jobs. At the best of times all the engines would be in fine condition, but in this picture from July 1961, when it was becoming increasingly difficult to find staff willing to work in the sheer dirt of a steam shed, standards were obviously falling. Not quite so perhaps with A4s Nos.60026 MILES BEEVOR, left, and the doyen of the class No.60014 SILVER LINK, centre, as they make ready to haul the named trains *THE HEART OF MIDLOTHIAN* and *THE TEES-THAMES* respectively. Sister A4 No.60033 SEAGULL is receiving attention to its smokebox and is in reasonable condition, but look at the sorry state of the pair of A3s, 34A's No.60063 ISINGLASS, second left, and with a scorched smokebox door, Gateshead depot's No.60045 LEMBERG, right. Both are filthy and carry NOT TO BE MOVED plates, indicating probably that they have somebody beneath them and are having to be worked upon in an effort to make them ready for traffic. These locomotives' fates, in numerical order, were: No.60014 built September 1935 and a long-term Kings Cross engine, withdrawn December 1962. No.60026 (Doncaster, February 1937) would move to New England in June 1963, then to Scotland four months later. There as part of a *renaissance* for the A4 locomotives based at Aberdeen Ferryhill, MILES BEEVOR (originally KESTREL was re-named in November 1947 for the chief legal advisor to the LNER 1943-1948), would see out its days to December 1965 sharing in the working of the Glasgow–Aberdeen 3-hour expresses. For No.60033 (Doncaster, June 1938), read as for 60014; a 34A engine for many years, withdrawn December 1962. No.60045 (carrying the name of the horse that won seventeen major races 1909–1911, including the 1910 Derby), was built in July 1924 and after this picture was taken, despite its external condition, would move several times between Gateshead, Heaton and Darlington sheds, before finishing a 40-year career at 51A in November 1964. Finally, No.60063 (between 1892 and 1895, the horse Isinglass won eleven of its twelve races, securing the 1893 English Triple Crown and winning a world record for those times, in prize money), came out of Doncaster in June 1925 and after leaving 34A in June 1963, would cease work four months later, based at New England. *THE HEART OF MIDLOTHIAN* ran King's Cross–Edinburgh–Perth, between 1951 and 1968, but *THE TEES-THAMES* (King's Cross–Middlesbrough–Saltburn) was very short-lived, running only during 1959–1961. So it is most fortuitous that this photograph captured a locomotive carrying that headboard. *A.R. Thompson (ARPT).*

A4 No.60003 ANDREW K. McKOSH poses in the afternoon sun of Sunday 28th October 1962, flanked by sisters Nos.60034 LORD FARINGDON (in the shed) and 60032 GANNET. No.60003 (Doncaster August 1937) was originally named OSPREY being re-named in October 1942 for Andrew K. McKosh, a Scottish industrialist and LNER board member. A long term King's Cross engine, 60003 would spend April to August 1957 based at Grantham, before returning to 34A to be withdrawn in December 1962.

No.60032 (Doncaster May 1938) was also a 34A based engine until the shed closed, when it transferred to New England in June 1963 to be retired four months later. No.60034 (Doncaster July 1938), named PEREGRINE, received the Peer's name in March 1948, to honour the famous stockbroker, who also was Chairman of the Great Central Railway and Deputy Chairman of the LNER. Another long term resident of Top Shed, 60034 left when the depot closed and found its way to Scotland where it took its place running the Glasgow–Aberdeen 3-hour trains, being withdrawn in August 1966. *K.H. Cockerill (ARPT).*

Peppercorn A1 No.60118 ARCHIBALD STURROCK looks somewhat unkempt on a gloomy day in March 1961. Built at Doncaster in November 1948 the Pacific went new to Copley Hill shed in Leeds and carries that depot's post-October 1956 shed code – 56C. The locomotive was based in the Leeds area for all its working life, leaving Copley Hill in November 1962 for Ardsley, moving on from there to Neville Hill, in July 1963; withdrawal came in October 1965. Archibald Sturrock became assistant to Daniel Gooch of Great Western Railway fame in 1840 and rose to become Manager of Swindon Works before joining the Great Northern Railway in 1850. He served until retiring in 1866, to be succeeded by Patrick Stirling. Alongside the A1 can be seen a very dirty L1 No.67794 (Robert Stephenson 7528/1950), which came to 34A in September 1958 from Grantham, only to return there in May 1961 and be taken out of service five months later. *C.J.B. Sanderson (ARPT).*

The east facing roads coming out of the eight-road building at 34A were perfect for getting perfectly side-lit portraits of engines, especially so in late afternoon when that most desirable of all – the 'back–lit glint'- could be had. Just such an opportunity was taken by Norman Preedy on Thursday 15th September 1960, when A4 No.60013 DOMINION OF NEW ZEALAND¸ in splendid condition, was standing by, ready for the off! The engine came out of Doncaster in June 1937 and by the beginning of British Railways, was based at Grantham, soon leaving there for Kings Cross; the Pacific remained at Top Shed for the rest of its career, to be withdrawn in April 1963. This superb portrait has but one flaw, in your scribe's opinion - the discarded bucket in the foreground, which keeps catching the eye! *Norman Preedy.*

Having just worked an Up express from West Yorkshire to London, A1 No.60148 ABOYEUR (Darlington, May 1949) comes under the York Way overbridge and heads for 34A's turntable, ash pits and coaling plant. The date: 28th April 1956, a Saturday, and the Pacific had been based at Copley Hill shed since moving there from Grantham on 28th August 1955. The engine would move on to Ardsley in September 1964 to work out its days until withdrawal on 21st June 1965. Aboyeur the racehorse found fame in 1913 when it won the Derby at the huge odds of 100/1! Shortly after it was sold to a Russian nobleman and disappeared in the upheaval of the 1917 Bolshevik Revolution. The tall building seen in the background is the London City Mission's Paget Memorial Hall in Randell's Road, which still stands today, a Grade II Listed structure. *C.J.B. Sanderson (ARPT).*

It is Wednesday 12th September 1962 and despite looking in pretty good order, Kings Cross A4 No.60028 WALTER K. WIGHAM has 108 more days until it was condemned on 29th December 1962. Named SEA EAGLE when it emerged from Doncaster in March 1937, the locomotive was re-named from 1st October 1947 for a former Director of a merchant bank and a member of the LNER's Board. Based at Grantham on 1st January 1948, No.60028 transferred to Kings Cross during the following May, to remain for the rest of its working life. After being condemned, the locomotive travelled light engine to Doncaster, entering the works on 18th January 1963 to be dismantled. *Norman Preedy.*

King's Cross – What was on shed Saturday 21st October 1956:
42374, 44911, 60003, 60007, 60015, 60017, 60021, 60022, 60025, 60026, 60029, 60030, 60033, 60055, 60109, 60121, 60130, 60134, 60149, 60151, 60157, 60508, 60800, 60826, 60849, 60855, 60861, 60869, 60871, 60902, 60903, 60914, 60917, 60943, 60950, 60983, 61093, 61200, 61203, 61287, 61311, 61331, 61364, 61838, 67741, 67751, 67761, 67773, 67774, 67779, 68855, 68862, 68888, 68966, 69491, 69492, 69493, 69495, 69496, 69497, 69498, 69499, 69506, 69512, 69517, 69523, 69527, 69528, 69529, 69532, 69535, 69538, 69539, 69540, 69541, 69543, 69544, 69545, 69546, 69548, 69549, 69559, 69568, 69570, 69572, 69573, 69575, 69576, 69577, 69579, 69583, 69584, 69585, 69589, 69590, 69593, 69635, 90096, 13159, 13160, 13161, 13162, 13165, 13166, 13306, 13307, 13308, 13309, 13310, 13312　　　　　　　　　　Total: 110.

King's Cross – What was on shed Sunday 25th February 1962:
60017, 60022, 60025, 60033, 60034, 60046, 60058, 60063, 60066, 60068, 60083, 60103, 60105, 60145, 60148, 60156, 60157, 60513, 60814, 60854, 60862, 60889, 60902, 60921, 60950, 60956, 60983, 61179, 61200, 61364, 61393, 61394, 61756, 67770, 67779, 67786, 67793, 67797, 67800, 69523, 69535, 69538, 69568, 69593, 90055, 90151, 90129, 92037, 92038, 92044, 92142, 92145, 92148, 92149, 92183, D347, D3307, D3310, D3715, D4083, D5644, D5677, D9009, D9011　　　　　　　　　　Total: 64.

This quintuple line-up from Saturday 8ᵗʰ November 1958 does not present much by way of spit-and polish or famous headboards; instead the engines have a workmanlike appearance, all ready for their next jobs, nevertheless. At right is 9F 2-10-0 No.92197 from Doncaster, to where it had been delivered, new, from Swindon works, just two months beforehand. No.92197 worked from Doncaster until February 1959 when it transferred to Frodingham to work steel traffic before reallocating again, in September 1960 to Immingham. There it remained until being withdrawn at the ludicrously early date of September 1965 – just seven years old! The other four engines did at least pay for themselves: A4 No.60026 MILES BEEVOR has already been discussed above; alongside is No.60007 SIR NIGEL GRESLEY, built in October 1937, and holder of a number of distinctions; the 100ᵗʰ Pacific to emerge from Doncaster; being named after its designer, and becoming, on 23ʳᵈ May 1959, BR's fastest steam locomotive with 112 m.p.h., hauling a special train. Working from King's Cross until closure of the depot, No.60007 moved to Scotland to work the Glasgow–Aberdeen express services. Withdrawn 1ˢᵗ February 1966, the Pacific was preserved and can be seen in action today. Next is No.60008 built Doncaster September 1937 as GOLDEN SHUTTLE, being re-named DWIGHT D. EISENHOWER in September 1945, in honour of the Supreme Commander of Allied Forces in Europe during WW2 and later to become President of the United States! The A4 worked from 34A until going to New England in June 1963 from where it was condemned the following month. Subsequently preserved No.60008 is today seen in The National Railway Museum, Green Bay, Wisconsin, USA. Lastly, we have V2 No.60924 of New England. The engine was built at Darlington in November 1941 and worked from New England until being reallocated to Doncaster in May 1962, being withdrawn sixteen months later. *I.S. Carr (ARPT).*

Met Shed: This picture gives a good idea of how the former carriage repair shop, itself once part of the original crescent locomotive shed, had been converted back into a seven-road depot for suburban tank engines – the 'Met Shed.' By the date of this picture, Thursday 23ʳᵈ March 1961, most of Kings Cross suburban duties had been taken over by diesel power, explaining the emptiness of what was once a very busy section of the depot, now with just a token N2 No.69546 in residence. Built April 1921 by the North British Locomotive Co. (Works No.22623), the condensing tank engine would be relocated to New England on 10ᵗʰ September 1961, from where it probably did little work and be condemned on 23ʳᵈ September 1962. Note the differing roof levels of the Met Shed. The five closest roads had been re-roofed for steam power whereas the furthest two roads had earlier been designated as the diesel shed for 0-6-0 shunting engines and retained the older northlight pattern roof. It was in the Met Shed that one of the last two K3 2-6-0s, No.61912 served as a stationary boiler after its arrival from Lincoln on 15ᵗʰ April 1962. Officially withdrawn on 16ᵗʰ September 1962, the K3 continued its boiler duty until June 1963, when it went to New England for further stationary boiler use, until finally ceasing all work in April 1965. Your scribe remembers the 2-6-0 well, in its tucked-away location in the Met Shed, where it was kept in surprisingly good external condition by the depot staff. *Norman Preedy.*

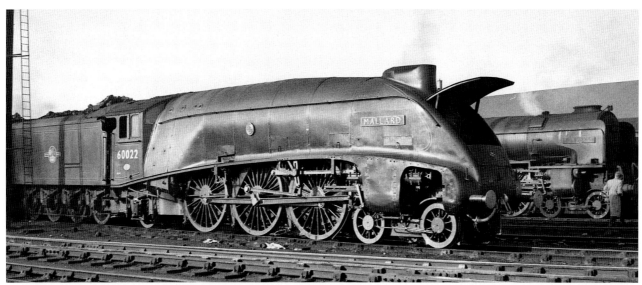

Back Pits (i) The late afternoon sun of Saturday 8th November 1958 nicely illuminates 34A's most famous locomotive – MALLARD – as it receives attention on the southernmost road of the Back Pits. A1 No.60155 BORDERER also basks in the sun, waiting to return to Tyneside and its home shed at Gateshead. Little need be said about the A4 which was built in March 1938 and worked from Kings Cross depot during BR times, to withdrawal on 25th April 1963 and subsequent preservation as part of the National Collection, at York NRM. Built Doncaster in September 1949, the A1 would transfer from 52A for nearby Heaton on 11th September 1960 and two years later relocate again to the Borders shed at Tweedmouth. Its stay at 52D was brief as in November 1962 No.60155 went south, on transfer to York, from where it was condemned on 4th October 1965. *I.S. Carr (ARPT).*

Back Pits (ii) Swindon-built in January 1958, BR Std. 9F No.92184 is just two months old as it rests in the Back Pits before working a freight train to the north. The date is Sunday 23rd March 1958 around the time when more freight engines would be seen at King's Cross as their usual haunt at Hornsey shed was converting to a diesel depot. No.92184 was allocated new to 35A New England which shed became 34E in February 1958; the 9F's shed plate has not yet been changed to the new code. It was also around this time that New England's men and 9F's were much in the news for incredible speed efforts. It started when an ailing Pacific came off its Up express at Grantham and all that depot had available was a New England 9F which then proceeded to haul the express to London, within the schedule and reaching 90 miles an hour when descending Stoke Bank! That opened the door for similar locomotive substitutions and the men made hay as they say, before 'authority' caught up with freight engines not only regularly reaching 90 m.p.h., but on at least one verified occasion, exceeding that velocity! Eventually officialdom formally put a stop to such antics, but *un*-officially, the 9Fs were still used on passenger workings at peak periods. It is not known if this particular locomotive was a 90 m.p.h. machine, but it was destined to have a criminally short life of just seven years, being withdrawn from Immingham in February 1965. *C.J.B. Sanderson (ARPT).*

Back Pits (iii) This image from Thursday 15th September 1960, illustrates a point about accuracy of records. It goes without saying that most railway enthusiasts are very punctilious – some even fanatical – about accuracy when dealing with any aspect of their hobby. One such very large matter is the thorny subject of locomotive allocations and their thousands of changes, every year; this is particularly a topic much in the news in some of the railway press of the present period. A3 No.60070 GLADIATEUR was, according to all available records, allocated to 56C Copley Hill shed in Leeds at the time, yet it carries a shed plate for 56B Ardsley! Alright, the two depots were not that far apart and it is known for a fact that locomotives were loaned unofficially between sheds, particularly those close-by, but it was exceeding rare for shed plates to be exchanged in such circumstances. But, that just may have happened in this instance, who knows? Built by the North British Locomotive Co. in Glasgow (No.23107), and put into traffic 24th September 1924, as LNER No.2569, the A1 was rebuilt to A3 standard at Doncaster at the end of 1946, emerging as No.70 on 18th January 1947. No.60070 *would* eventually become an Ardsley engine, transferring there from 56C in September 1961. Further allocation changes were June 1963 to Neville Hill and then in December 1963 to Gateshead, followed by withdrawal in May 1964. Gladiateur the horse was a French thoroughbred that won the English Triple Crown in 1865 and many races in its own country in that year and the following. *C.J.B. Sanderson (ARPT).*

Back Pits (iv) An action-packed picture from the Back Pits on Thursday 22nd February 1962; note the innovative overhead watering gantry. The locomotives seen, from left to right: an unidentified A3, V2 No.60841 from New England, then Peppercorn A1 No.60128 BONGRACE from Doncaster, but missing its shed plate, and V2 No.60862; at right, the Silver Fox adornment identifies A4 No.60017; the last two were 34A locomotives. No.60841 (Darlington, November 1938) would reallocate to Doncaster in June 1963 and be condemned three months later. No.60128 (Doncaster, May 1949) would remain at 36A until condemned on 10th January 1965. The horse for which the engine was named was born in 1923 and counted among its forebears such legends as Spion Kop, Spearmint and Vaucluse; it won many races in the USA. V2 No.60862 (Darlington, June 1939) would transfer from King's Cross on 21st April 1963 for New England, being condemned during the following June. The word 'iconic' is perhaps over-used when it comes to the A4s, but certainly it could apply to No.60017 SILVER FOX, star of the superb 1954 documentary film *Elizabethan Express* and as far as your scribe is concerned, one of the East Coast Pacifics that hauled a train on which he was travelling, at over 100 m.p.h! That was the Locomotive Club of Great Britain's *GREAT NORTHERN* rail tour of Saturday 19th May 1962, from London to Doncaster and return in 2 hours and 35 minutes, non-stop, each way – i.e, a 60 m.p.h. timing. A3 No.60066 MERRY HAMPTON got the train to Doncaster dead on time, with 92 m.p.h. near Hitchin, while on the return, No.60017 arrived at King's Cross three minutes early, with 102½ m.p.h. attained approaching Essendine. Marvellous performances by both engines! But their time was limited, with condemnations following for Nos.60066 and 60017 in September and October 1963, respectively. *Norman Preedy.*

Back Pits (v) Mainstay of the Kings Cross suburban services from their introduction in 1920, until the coming of diesels in the late 1950s, the N2 class 0-6-2T would eventually total 107 locomotives of which 84 were fitted with condensing apparatus for working through underground lines. Fifty-seven of the class were on Top Shed's roster on the first day of BR and two of them are seen here on the Back Pits in the summer of 1955. No.69541 (NBL 22618/1921) would work from 34A until withdrawal in August 1959, while No.69573 (Hawthorn Leslie 3696 of November 1928) would be retired in November 1958. More memories for your scribe who well remembers the N2's blasting out of the underground line from Moorgate, with their train of two, Quad-Art sets, to halt at the single platform serving that line. Then came the start on the steep gradient with invariably greasy rails – 'volcanic' is a word that comes to mind, so much so that some trains were double-headed, one regular working in particular with a Class B1 that came off the adjacent locomotive yard and piloted the N2 past the yard and into Gasworks Tunnel. *K.H. Cockerill (ARPT).*

Back Pits (vii) MALLARD – this time on 8th November 1958 – and looking splendid following a General overhaul between the 21st July and 27th August last. The engine sits at the western end of the Back Pits sidings from where a good view is obtained of how the 1851 crescent shed had been re-roofed with partially new side walls at the rear. Alongside No.60022 is A1 No.60144 KING'S COURIER from Doncaster depot, a locomotive built at Darlington in March 1949. The A1 would stay at 36A until condemned in April 1963. The racehorse for which the engine was named came out of Kingston and Stylitene, both American thoroughbreds, before moving to England. There, King's Courier made thirty starts, winning twelve, including the 1900 Doncaster Cup and being 'placed' in two. *Alf York.*

In early June 1963, A2/3 No.60500 EDWARD THOMPSON is seen at 34A's coaling area with the huge coaling tower dominating the scene; this could well be the last picture of No.60500 in service as it was condemned on 16th June 1963. Named after its designer the locomotive had been built at Doncaster in May 1946 and spent most of its BR service at New England shed, Peterborough. It is popular legend that generally, the Thompson A2 classes were not much liked and some of the sub-classes were indeed not particularly good. But, on form, they were very powerful machines and spent a lot of their time working heavy overnight sleeping car trains and, at least one them – A2/3 No.60520 OWEN TUDOR – was recorded at 100 m.p.h. descending Stoke Bank; so, they were not *all* bad! *A. Ives (ARPT)*.

Class J52 (GNR Class J13) No.68846, reallocated to King's Cross shed from Hornsey on 22nd February 1959. It was still carrying a Hornsey shed plate when photographed near the coaling plant on a gloomy Wednesday 6th May 1959. The engine's superb condition was no accident because next day, Thursday 7th May 1959, was Ascension Day, when the J52 would leave King's Cross on a two-coach special train to Marshmoor, Hertfordshire. There it would be handed over to Captain Bill Smith RNR (retired), who had purchased the locomotive, the very first of what would be many, to be sold out of BR service. Built in 1899 at the Atlas Works, Glasgow of Sharp Stewart (Works No.4492) as GNR 1247, the engine became LNER 4247, then 8846 from 15th December 1946, before BR added the prefix 6 on 28th December 1948. Eventually the J52 would be donated to the NRM, from where it has worked on preserved railway lines around Britain, through two boiler certifications. Today, this historic engine is a static display exhibit. Also seen A4 No.60006 SIR RALPH WEDGWOOD and just behind 68846, Kings Cross-allocated B1 No.61075. *I.S. Carr (ARPT)*.

These two images from Thursday 15th September 1960 are perfect reminders of the super condition in which some East Coast depots kept at least some of their locomotives. With its crew all smiles, Grantham shed's A3 No.60065 KNIGHT OF THISTLE (NBL 23102/1924), looks absolutely splendid on 34A's turntable, the engine's appearance greatly enhanced (in the writer's opinion) by the Kylchap double chimney and German-style smoke deflectors. Not quite so good looking, but handsome nevertheless in classic rods-down pose, is King's Cross' own Kylchap-fitted V2 No.60903 (Darlington, March 1940), in well-groomed green livery. No.60065 would leave Grantham in June 1962 for New England, only to return exactly a year later. The Pacific then transferred to Doncaster on 8th September 1963 before going yet again to New England on 20th October 1963 where it was condemned on 28th June 1964. The V2 would remain at 34A until 27th January 1963 leaving also for New England where it was condemned on the 10th day of the next month. Both engines were being turned under vacuum power on the depot's 70 foot, 165 tons capacity turntable of the Mundt-type, provided by Ransomes & Rapier Ltd, of Ipswich. (The Mundt turntable features three-point support – the centre pivot and both ends' carrying wheels – thereby obviating the need for balancing the load). The four-legged Knight of Thistle was foaled in 1893 out of Roseberry and The Empress Maud, would win several big races in Britain including the Royal Hunt Cup, before being taken to the USA where he sired a later winner of the Kentucky Derby. More memories for the author here: at left, on the skyline, is a North London Railway signal box. Below that is a ramp that led from gates in York Way – the road seen crossing the railway behind the turntable. Set into those gates was a 'Judas Door' which was not locked on Sundays, thereby allowing clandestine visitors to the shed to sneak down the ramp to the rear of the Back Pits and from there it was fingers crossed! Happy days…! *Both, C.J.B. Sanderson (ARPT).*

HORNSEY

Hornsey's first engine shed was a small two road dead-end building on the east side of the first station, opened in August 1850, with the GNR main line. That shed lasted until about 1866, when station rearrangements required its removal; it was replaced by a similarly sized building at Wood Green, (closed 1899).

In 1899, an eight road, dead-end brick building with a northlight roof was erected on built-up ground on the east side of Hornsey station. It had the usual turntable and ramped coaling stage and immediately took over the duties of dealing with freight engines and the many, smaller locomotives involved with trip and shunting work; some of Kings Cross shed's suburban passenger work moved to Hornsey also.

In 1928 the LNER provided a mechanical coaling plant and an enlarged turntable. HSY was the shed code given by the LNER, changed to 34B by BR. The ER also had a major job to do when the 1921 refurbished northlight roof again became degraded. So, in 1955 the unusual task of changing a shed's roof design came about, and an entirely new roof of transverse pitches was fitted.

Hornsey was significant in 1958 when it became the first (partial) ECML diesel depot in London; this was until a purpose-built diesel shed was opened at Finsbury Park in April 1960. Following that Hornsey closed to steam in June 1961 when its remaining locomotives were reallocated to various ex-GNR sheds. After King's Cross shed closed, steam had again to come to Hornsey for turning and watering while any necessary coaling was carried out at King's Cross station's locomotive stabling point – 'Bottom Shed'. 34B was fully closed in 1971. Today a substantial portion of the shed still exists, incorporated into an electric multiple unit depot.

With the King's Cross shed just under three miles away, and an allocation of a few 0-6-0s and lots of 0-6-0 tank engines for shunting and 0-6-2 tanks for suburban passenger services, it is little wonder that Hornsey engine shed was not so often visited and photographed. Seen on Sunday 22nd September 1957, and despite being only a few months away from becoming a predominantly diesel locomotive shed, Hornsey still presented a typical vista of N2 and J50 tank locos, several of which may be identified: N2 No.69522, a Hornsey resident along with sister No.69501 which might have been out of use. In the distance by the old coaling stage and the depot's 15-ton capacity Cowans Sheldon, steam breakdown crane, are J50s Nos.68920, and 68991. Such engines spent their days shunting and trip working, some of which duties took them south of the Thames. *Norman Preedy.*

Hornsey – What was on shed Saturday 12th July 1952:
61091, 64256, 64678, 64679, 64684, 64699, 67756, 67775, 68758, 68759, 68760, 68761, 68770, 68773, 68776, 68777, 68778, 68781, 68784, 68791, 68793, 68794, 68796, 68808, 68811, 68815, 68825, 68826, 68833, 68834, 68851, 68856, 68873, 68949, 69431, 69433, 69441, 69445, 69455, 69457, 69458, 69460, 69467, 69468, 69469, 69470, 69477, 69481, 69492, 69505, 69513, 69533, 69547, 69556, 69567, 69613, 90088, 90165, 90191, 90454, 90526, 12112   Total: 62.

(opposite, top) Hornsey saw its fair share of WD 2-8-0 comings and goings but the depot only ever had seven of the class allocated throughout the BR period, two for a couple of weeks during the late summer of 1948 – Nos.90002 and 90490 – and then five others in 1960 – 90129, 90156, 90480, 90502, and 90660 – one stayed for three weeks in January, whilst the others put in stints of fourteen to fifteen months into June and July 1961; all this during a period when diesel locomotives were descending on to London in their droves, particularly around Hornsey and neighbourhood. This image reveals three WD 'Austerities' stabled alongside the shed on Sunday 11ᵗʰ December 1960 with visiting No.90151 from New England to the fore. The eagle-eyed amongst you will have noted that the unidentified WD behind our subject has a question mark chalked onto the smokebox door where a shed plate normally sits. *Les Waters coll.*

(opposite, centre) During a visit to the shed on Sunday 15ᵗʰ February 1959, the photographer was astute enough to log the locomotives appearing in this rather murky – but nevertheless atmospheric and time of the year (not to mention the century) when such weather conditions prevailed and were expected – picture. Anyway, for those interested, the numbers were, left to right: a BRC&W Type 2 D53xx diesel-electric (D5300 to D5315 were already resident at 34B so it could have been any of those), EE Type 4 D209, allocated to Hornsey since new on 15ᵗʰ September 1958; it was soon to depart for a new home on the other side of the main line at the dedicated depot being built at Finsbury Park. Next is our line of J50s which consisted of: Nos.68946 (leading), 68930, 68894, 68985, 68917, 68986, 68966, and 68931. Note where all the hordes of visiting spotters were heading – towards the diesels! *Les Waters coll.*

(opposite, bottom) Besides the stabling of diesels in the shed yard, sidings on the periphery of the depot were also used to stable the expanding diesel fleet. On the higher ground on the west side of the shed two siding were dedicated to refuelling the diesels and in this scene from 1959, a pair of those 'Baby Deltic's' D5908 and D5907 are quietly minding their own business. They look very new and clean so the date of the image must have been June 1959 just after D5908 had been put into traffic. Although the class consisted just ten locomotives (a blessing surely), they courted controversy from day one when on delivery to Doncaster for acceptance trials, D5900 and D5901 were found to be overweight and were sent back to Vulcan Foundry. Sister D5902 was still at Newton-le-Willows virtually ready for delivery so she had to be taken back into the factory and parts of the bodywork cut away in order to comply. D5903 and D5904 were not so well advanced in the erecting process so it was easier to shave some weight off them, likewise D5905 and D5906. The first of the class to be put into traffic were D5903 and D5904 on 22ⁿᵈ April 1959; the others followed as 02 on 1ˢᵗ May, 05 and 06 on 8ᵗʰ May, 07 on 15ᵗʰ May, 00 and 01 came on 22ⁿᵈ May, 08 on 29ᵗʰ May, and 09 on 16ᵗʰ June. And then the trouble started! *I.S.Carr (ARPT).*

J50, WD 2-8-0, L1, N2, J50; and so they were lined-up on 23ʳᵈ March 1961! They could have all been 34B engines, quite a variety for so late on. No.68971 is a steam brake version of the J50 class and was of no use whatsoever for passenger stock work – goods yards and trip freights were its lot in life; the rest of them are unidentified but no matter, they look good in steam awaiting their next call of duty. A question I ask whenever I see accumulations of ash and clinker just dumped on the ground in these yards is at what stage would the ground surrounding the rails begin to project higher than the rails themselves? Labour in post-war Britain and London in particular became very scarce and attracting anyone to these dirty conditions with their seemingly parallel low wages was eventually a non-starter. The joys of steam! *Norman Preedy.*

The number of N7s allocated to Hornsey could be counted on your fingers – six is the answer and not all at once! Two came in LNER times, No.456 (69625) arrived new from Gorton on 20th October 1925 but on 17th December 1928 it transferred to Stratford. Just over a year later No.457 (69626) transferred from Hatfield on 4th March 1930 but on 12th December it was parcelled off to Stratford as another Christmas present. Many years passed and N7s became as rare as chickens teeth at Hornsey until somebody at the fairly new British Railways looked at the lists and decided 34B needed an N7! And so on the 20th November 1955 No.69618 arrived from Stratford; as if realising that Hornsey had given Stratford two early Xmas presents many years beforehand, 30A sent No.69629 on Christmas Day 1955, according to the record. Both 1955 acquisitions transferred to Hatfield in February 1959. But that wasn't the end of it because in the interim No.69612 transferred in from Stratford on 10th June 1956 but was gone a year later to Colchester. On 18th May 1958 No.69637 turned up from Hatfield but at the end of the following March it was condemned. That was the last of the connections with N7s. On 22nd September 1958 No.69618 stands amongst the debris from fire and smokebox cleaning, and bunker trimming too by the size of that coal hill! We haven't had any reports of how these 0-6-2Ts were received at 34B so we can't really pass comment. *Norman Preedy*.

Third world!? Banana republic!? Neither, this is Hornsey towards the end of steam. Bit of a mess! J50s rule just now or should that be diesels? No.68970 and 68990 have both lost their shed plates and as for cleaning! Note that one of them has vacuum ejector for carriage working whereas the other just has steam brakes. No.68970 came to Hornsey on 26th October 1958 from Doncaster but never returned – to work – and was condemned 19th April 1961 after attending 'The Plant' for repair; it was then cut-up. No.68990 was one of the Gorton-built batch and was put into traffic with vacuum brakes, it transferred to Hornsey 19th October 1952 from Darnall. It too went to Doncaster in April 1961 for repair but was condemned on the 21st. We must be somewhere near those dates now. *Les Waters coll*.

The western wall of Hornsey shed on 18th August 1950 when northlights still held sway and rebuilding was some years off. Resident J52 No.68827 looks into the turntable pit whilst its crew take afternoon tea. *C.W. Allen (ARPT)*.

Even when the roof rebuilding work was being undertaken, the yard was used for stabling. The contractors were certainly up against it whereby the scaffolding was fixed to fit the loading gauge to enable locomotives to ease onto the sidings – no carte' blanche' here. The date is 8th May 1955 and work is proceeding nicely to get the brickwork in place. *F.W. Hampson (ARPT)*.

Just a month before it was condemned, No.68990 is unceremoniously dumped near the turntable. This image enables us to see the transition in the roof line between the stabling shed and the stores/offices section of the shed which kept its northlight roof. The new roof-level walkway design has taken a leaf out of the scaffolding erectors' books! *C.J.B. Sanderson (ARPT)*.

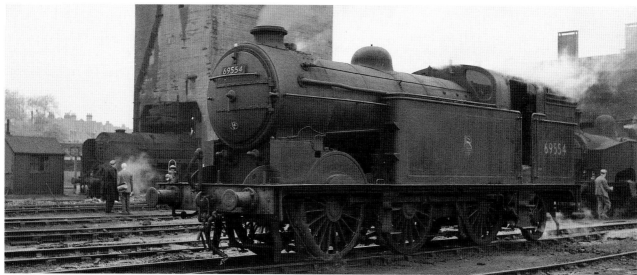

Hornsey's coaling plant was one of the early examples erected by the LNER and its architecture was something of a one-off because it's like was never seen again in Britain. A BR Std.9F is taking coal prior to turning whilst resident N2 No.69554 simmers on the shed yard after a day out. The date is 18th May 1957, a Saturday, and the shed yard will start to slowly fill up with locomotives completing their duties. The ground it will be noted is sodden with water, oil, and contaminated liquids. It would either burn extremely well or contaminate a water course if left to its own devices (wasn't the New River close by, behind the shed?). *C.J.B. Sanderson (ARPT)*.

Long after steam had left the premises and the diesels were using the place as an annexe of Finsbury Park, steam from faraway places used to visit London and of course they required turning. The only place left with a turntable at this end of the ECML was Hornsey and so A4 No.60009 UNION OF SOUTH AFRICA took advantage of the asset on Friday 23rd October 1964. The 160-tons of A4 and tender are being helped manually to turn as the vacuum tractor appears to be 'playing-up' just when it shouldn't! No.60009 would be making history when working the last steam hauled train out of King's Cross station the following day. Allocated to Aberdeen Ferryhill since 20th May 1962, No.60009 was withdrawn from 61B on 1st June 1966 and sold into preservation the following month. The tender behind UOSA here was number 5332, a corridor tender which would have gone with the A4 into preservation but in April 1966 the owner of FLYING SCOTSMAN, Alan Pegler, paid BR £800 for it. That then left BR in a bit of a pickle because when J.B. Cameron paid them for 60009 and its tender, the original wasn't now available so in order to fulfil their commitment, BR sold corridor tender No.5484 with the A4. That tender had come off A4 No.60004 but had been built for the W1 class 4-6-4 No.10000 (the 'Hush-Hush') in 1929. Plenty of history there then! Okay, nearly there! Well, half way, nearly! The shiny rails in the foreground belong to the diesel fuelling point which it appears has plenty of customers. *Les Waters coll*.

Hornsey – What was on shed Sunday 24th May 1959:

61027, 64196, 64223, 64233, 64253, 68033, 68067, 68073, 68075, 68077, 68891, 68894, 68917, 68918, 68926, 68928, 68930, 68931, 68936, 68945, 68946, 68960, 68961, 68966, 68968, 68970, 68971, 68972, 68979, 68980, 68981, 68982, 68983, 68986, 68987, 68989, 68990, 69505, 69513, 69522, 69533, 69536, 69556, 69560, 69561, 69571, 69572, 69594, 90096, 90151, 90246, 90253, 90269, 90659, 90665, 92141, 92188, D206, 12129, 12131, 12137, 12138, 13331, 13332, D3691, D3692, D5300, D5302, D5303, D5304, D5306, D5309, D5311, D5315, D5318, D5902, D5907, D6100, D6101, D6105, D6108, DELTIC   Total: 82.